SAINT ROSE
OF LIMA

SAINT ROSE OF LIMA

THE STORY OF THE FIRST CANONIZED SAINT OF THE NEW WORLD

By
Mary Fabyan Windeatt

Illustrated by
Sister Mary Jean, O.P.

TAN BOOKS AND PUBLISHERS, INC.
Rockford, Illinois 61105

Nihil Obstat: Henry J. Zolzer
                  Censor

Imprimatur: ✠ Thomas H. McLaughlin
                  Bishop of Paterson
                  October 15, 1943

The greater part of this book originally appeared in the pages of *The Torch*. This book was formerly titled *Angel of the Andes: The Story of Saint Rose of Lima*.

ISBN: 0-89555-424-0

Library of Congress Catalog Card No.: 93-83096

Printed and bound in the United States of America.

TAN BOOKS AND PUBLISHERS, INC.
P.O. Box 424
Rockford, Illinois 61105

1993

For
Sister Rose Celestine
of the
Sisters of Charity of Saint Vincent de Paul,
Halifax, Nova Scotia.

CONTENTS

ACKNOWLEDGMENTS

The author wishes to thank Reverend Norbert Georges, O.P., Director of the Blessed Martin Guild, and Miss Dora Vigors of Lima, Peru, for much valuable information concerning the life and times of Saint Rose of Lima—Patroness and first canonized Saint of the New World.

CHAPTER 1

WHAT'S IN A NAME?

I T WAS a July day in the city of Lima, with the sun hiding behind the thick blanket of mist which generally covers the coasts of Peru and Chile from June until September. Maria de Oliva Flores shivered as she went out into the large garden behind her house. Such days as these, with no sunlight, did not please her. The air was heavy and damp. She felt like sleeping all the time.

"Marianna! Are you out here?"

From the other end of the garden, out of sight among the trees and flowers, came a girl's voice.

"*Sí, señora.* I am with little Isabel."

Maria de Oliva turned into a narrow path, bending her head as she passed under a spreading fig tree. She might have known. Marianna, the Indian servant girl, always came out here after lunch with the baby of the Flores family. Three-month-old Isabel was definitely Marianna's favorite. Now Maria quickened her steps as she came to where Marianna was sitting beside the child's cradle. There was a proud smile on her face as she lifted

1

the lace covering and looked down at her youngest child.

"Marianna, I've had many children, but I believe Isabel is the sweetest of all. Such pretty dark hair and eyes! And those little pink cheeks. . ."

The young Indian girl smiled, her white teeth flashing in the bronze of her face. "Isabel is like a flower, *señora*. And so good! I've never seen such a lovely baby."

"Like a flower, Marianna? What flower?"

"A rose, *señora*. A beautiful pink rose. Just look at her now, smiling at us as though she knew what we were saying!"

Maria de Oliva was quiet a moment. This child had been born three months ago—on April 30, the feast of Saint Catherine of Siena. On May 25 she had been baptized by Father Anthony Polanco at the Church of San Sebastián and given the name Isabel. This had been to please her grandmother, Isabel de Herrera, Maria de Oliva's own mother. But did that name really suit the child? Wouldn't it be better to call her Rose, after the flower she resembled so much?

Marianna busied herself with her mending. The Flores family was not wealthy. With several children to feed and clothe, Gaspar Flores could afford only one servant. That meant Marianna had little free time. But she did not mind; now that little Isabel had come, it was especially good to be part of the Flores household.

"When this baby grows up, she will be the prettiest girl in Lima," said Marianna. "She will bring us good luck."

"We can use it," sighed Maria. "Sometimes it's a very hard struggle to make ends meet. Let's hope that Rose marries a wealthy man."

"Rose, *señora?*"

"That's right. I'm not going to call her Isabel any more. Rose suits her better. I know her grandmother won't mind if we change it."

Isabel de Herrera did mind, however. Her pride had been greatly flattered when Maria de Oliva had named her pretty little daughter after her, and she refused to hear of a change.

"She was called Isabel in Baptism, Maria. Why do you want to alter things now?"

"Because I think the name of Rose is better suited to her. Mother, please don't make things difficult for me!"

Isabel de Herrera had a hot temper. "*Difficult?* What are you talking about? The child's name is Isabel. That's all there is to it!"

"It's Rose!"

"It's Isabel!"

"Rose, I tell you!"

"Isabel!"

Sometimes Gaspar Flores lost patience with his wife and mother-in-law. "Call the child anything you like," he pleaded, "only let a man have some peace in his own house. *Please!*"

One year passed, two years, four years, and still the small Flores child was the center of a bitter struggle.

"It's certainly very foolish," said the neighbors.

"That poor little girl is afraid to answer to Rose because it displeases her grandmother. And she doesn't know what to do when anyone calls her Isabel because then her mother is angry. Why doesn't Gaspar put his foot down?"

But Gaspar Flores felt powerless. He felt that he could do little with his wife, much less with his mother-in-law.

"God help us all!" he often prayed.

One day Maria de Oliva, who was given to sudden fits of energy, decided to teach her little girl to read and write.

"Rose, you're nearly five years old. I think you could learn the alphabet. Look—this is the letter A. This one is B. And here is C. It's really very simple."

Rose found a piece of paper and some colored chalk. This was going to be nice! Bernardina, her oldest sister, knew all about reading and writing. So did Jane and Andrew and Anthony and Matthew. Even seven-year-old Ferdinand could write his name quite well. Perhaps, thought Rose, she could catch up with her brothers and sisters if she worked hard.

After half an hour of copying letters, however, Rose's small fingers grew stiff.

"I'm tired and so are you," announced Maria de Oliva. "We'll have another lesson tomorrow. Now I want you to promise me something."

"Yes, Mother?"

"You're not to answer to any other name but Rose. No—it doesn't matter if your grandmother is cross. Your name is Rose Flores and nothing else. Understand?"

Rose nodded. The trouble about her name had always made her sad. She hated to see people quarreling, particularly her mother and grandmother. Ever since she could remember, however, there had been arguments between the two. Even though Maria insisted that she had once had a vision in which she saw a beautiful pink rose floating over Rose's cradle, Isabel de Herrera would not believe it.

"That rose was a sign from Heaven telling me to change the child's name," said Maria de Oliva. "I'm absolutely convinced of it."

"A sign from Heaven, indeed!" the older woman cried out. "It was nothing but your own imagination!"

Maria soon grew tired of teaching her small daughter to read and write. She didn't have much patience, even at the best of times. And there was no one else to be interested in the child's great desire to learn.

"You're only a very little girl," Marianna comforted her one day. "There's plenty of time for you to learn reading and writing. As far as that goes, people can be quite happy without knowing how to do either of them. There's just one thing that's really important."

"What?" asked Rose eagerly.

"Knowing what is good and doing it. You'll never have any real trouble if you remember that, my child."

Marianna's words pleased Rose and she often turned them over in her mind. God was good. The more one thought about Him, the better one came to know Him. After that, being good and doing good were the simplest things in the world. Still, though, it would be nice to know a few things so that one might be useful to other people.

"I'm going to pray," the little girl told herself. "Since no one has time to teach me things, I'm going to ask God to do it. He can do anything, can't He?"

Maria de Oliva had a statue of the Christ Child in her room. As was the Peruvian custom, the statue had a robe of its very own. This one was of red velvet with gold trimmings. Every day Rose knelt down before the little statue and said a prayer.

"Lord, help me to know and love You," she said very softly. "And please teach me to read and write!"

Maria de Oliva didn't know about these little prayers of Rose's. She had a lot to do to run her big house, and sometimes the work made her tired and cross.

"It won't always be like this," she thought. "Someday the children will marry, perhaps quite well. Then I'll be able to take things easier."

One morning Maria was baking bread. The kitchen was hot and steamy, and she was not in the mood to talk to anyone.

"Don't bother me now," she said, as Rose pushed open the door. "Go and play with Ferdinand until

"MOTHER, I KNOW HOW TO READ AND WRITE!"

dinner time."

"But Mother! Don't you want to hear something wonderful? I know how to read and write!"

Maria de Oliva pounded the big mound of dough before her. "You mustn't make up stories," she said. "You're not a baby anymore. You ought to know that to tell a lie is a sin."

"I'm not telling a lie, Mother. I know how to read and write! Really and truly! Look!"

Maria glanced at the paper which Rose held out to her. It was covered with words, neatly written in a large round hand. For a five-year-old child, the writing was very good.

"Someone's been helping you!" she said, a little sharply. "Your father or your grandmother."

Rose shook her head. "Nobody helped me, Mother. Only the little Christ Child. You're always so busy I didn't want to bother you, so I just asked Him to help me. And He did!"

Some of the flush faded from Maria's heated face. "Go and bring me a book," she ordered sternly. "Any book. We'll soon see if you're telling the truth."

In a few minutes Rose was back with a big green volume. "Look, Mother, there are four words in gold letters on the cover. I can read every one of them."

Maria de Oliva stared. If this child of hers was really telling the truth. . . .

"Well? What are those four words?"

Rose smiled. This was a wonderful day. She would remember it as long as she lived. The four golden words on the cover of the green book were SAINT CATHERINE OF SIENA. Inside there were many more words, telling the life story of the great Italian saint upon whose feast day she had been born. And she could read every one of them!

CHAPTER 2

COME, HOLY GHOST!

THERE WAS much excitement in the Flores household at the news that five-year-old Rose had learned to read and write. No one seemed inclined to believe, however, that the Infant Jesus had been her teacher.

"Some youngsters have too much imagination," declared Maria de Oliva. "I'm afraid our Rose is one of them."

"You mean *Isabel*, don't you?" said her mother pointedly. "That's her real name. As for me, I feel there may be some truth in what she says. After all, who can say what God will do for a little child who loves Him?"

As the months passed, the incident was almost forgotten. When it was remembered, people said it was less a matter of prayer than of natural skill. Rose Flores was a clever child. She had simply picked up reading and writing by herself, the way she had picked up music. Couldn't she play little tunes on the guitar and harp? Hadn't she been heard singing her own verses, down at the back of the garden, when she thought no one was around? The whole thing was so simple. There had been no miracle, really. The child was just naturally bright.

Rose knew the truth, however. Of herself she was nothing—God was everything. She would never forget that. She would ask His help all through her life. He would listen to her, as He had done about the reading and writing, just because she was so weak and helpless.

Time passed. Rose had her sixth birthday, her eighth, her tenth. By now there were eleven children in the Flores family. The big house on the street named after Saint Dominic, the Street of Santo Domingo, was a very crowded place. Rose's father, Gaspar Flores, who had come to Lima several years ago from Puerto Rico, was finding it hard to support his large family. Of course he did have a job: for some time he had been in charge of making guns and other weapons for the royal Spanish armies stationed in Lima. It was a fair position, given to him by Don Andrés Hurtado de Mendoza, Viceroy of Peru. But what a lot of worry eleven children could be! How much it took to feed and clothe them!

One day in the year 1597 Gaspar sought out his wife. He had just been offered the chance to take charge of a silver mine at Quivi, a small mountain town not far from Lima.

"There's more money in mining than in anything else," he told Maria. "I'll go to Quivi for a few months to see how things go. If I don't like the work, I can always come back to the old job."

"Are you sure?"

Gaspar laughed. "Of course I'm sure. Everyone knows the swords and guns I make are the best to be found in Peru."

Maria thought long about the news. In the end she informed Gaspar she was coming with him to Quivi. "It will be wonderful to live in the mountains," she said. "We all need a change from city life."

The man frowned. "Suppose this new job doesn't turn out well?"

"Didn't you just tell me you make the best guns and swords? That the Viceroy is pleased with your work? Nonsense, Gaspar! I'll go now and see to the packing."

And so it came about that the Flores family said good-bye to the big rambling house in Lima and went off to Quivi. Rose, now eleven years old, was very excited at the change. For the first time in her life she was close to the great mountains that stood back of her native city. A few miles to the west rolled the green waters of the Pacific, breaking in white foam along endless miles of sand. As the journey progressed, little Indian villages came into view, the houses made of light-brown clay and roofed with red and yellow tile.

Ferdinand, Rose's favorite brother, was also interested in the new sights. He liked the strange animals the Indians had—the llamas with their long necks, the little silky vicuñas, the alpacas with their shaggy brown coats. These odd-looking beasts were to be seen everywhere, grazing on the grassy slopes of the Andes or bearing burdens for their Indian masters.

"I wish I had a llama," Ferdinand told his sister. "I could teach him tricks and Marianna could cut his fur and weave it into nice warm clothes. That would save Father quite a bit of money."

Rose agreed. Ferdinand always had good ideas. "Maybe I could do something to help, too," she said. "What would it be, though?"

The boy wrinkled his brow. There wasn't much a Peruvian girl could do. Daughters of the better families either married or entered a convent. They never went out in the world to make a living.

"Why worry about such things? Mother says you're going to marry a wealthy man when you grow up."

Sudden tears filled Rose's dark eyes. "I don't want to get married, Ferdinand. I just want to stay home and be useful there."

The thirteen-year-old boy laughed. He was proud of his pretty young sister, even if she did say strange things sometimes.

There was a small church at Quivi. The Flores family visited it soon after their arrival and found the parish priest, Father Francis Gonzalez, greatly excited. Word had just been received that the Archbishop of Lima was coming to give the Sacrament of Confirmation.

"That's fine," said Maria de Oliva. "I have a little girl who hasn't been confirmed yet. We'll start to get her ready."

"I hope she knows her prayers," said Ferdinand.

"I WISH I HAD A LLAMA,"
FERDINAND TOLD HIS SISTER.

"Do you, Rose? The Archbishop will ask you lots of questions. He can't bring the Holy Ghost into your soul unless you know your Catechism."

"Ferdinand, don't tease your sister!" cried Maria de Oliva. "Of course Rose will know her Catechism. I'll see to that myself."

So every day Rose studied her Catechism. It was a little book written by the Archbishop himself, and printed in 1584, the first volume to see the light of day in South America. Rose's copy was written in the Spanish language, but the good Archbishop had also compiled two other Catechisms, one in Quechua and one in Aymará, two dialects common among the Indians.

Those who knew Archbishop Turribius were quite sure he was a saint. His full name was Turribius Alphonsus de Mogrovejo, and he had come to Lima in 1581 to be the second Archbishop of the city. Like the first Archbishop, Jerome de Loaysa, the famous Dominican, Turribius was a Spaniard. His official residence stood next to the cathedral, across from the Plaza de Armas. This Plaza was Lima's most beautiful park. Here the people would spend many hours enjoying the colorful flowers and the shade of the graceful palms. But whenever the Archbishop was seen coming from his house, everybody in the Plaza rushed forward to receive his blessing. Beggars and cripples were especially eager, for in the past the good man's prayers had worked many a marvel for the poor and the sick.

Although Gaspar's young daughter was very excited about the approaching visit of the Archbishop, the other people in Quivi were not. Most of the town's three thousand inhabitants were Indians who spoke the Quechua dialect. They were still a long way from being Christianized, these Indians; the true Faith was unfortunately linked in their minds with the band of ruthless soldiers from across the Atlantic Ocean who, in 1532, had swept down upon the country and claimed it for the King of Spain.

It was Francisco Pizarro who had led these new-comers, and with him had come misfortune for the natives. Their lands had been seized, and they had been forced to work in the mines for miserable wages. Franciscan and Dominican priests from Spain followed in Pizarro's wake, bringing the great gift of the Faith, but the Indians did not realize that the Spanish soldier represented one thing and the Spanish priest another. To most of the Indians, a Spaniard was someone to be feared and distrusted, no matter what his calling.

Rose was surprised to find she was the only girl in the church on the day of Confirmation. There were two small boys, however, and the three children knelt in the sanctuary before the Archbishop of Lima. Sun flooded the interior of the little church, falling on the golden mitre of the Arch-bishop and on the magnificent ring he wore upon his right hand. What a wonderful day this was! And what a pity the people in Quivi did not realize it. By rights, thought Rose, the church should be crowded.

The Archbishop was a small, rather slight man,

fifty-nine years of age. He sat in a chair before the three kneeling children and explained what was about to take place. The Holy Ghost, the Third Person of the Most Blessed Trinity, was going to come into their souls. He would stay there as long as those souls did not offend God seriously, by mortal sin. That would be forever, wouldn't it?

"Forever," said the two little boys.

"Forever and ever," said Rose.

The Archbishop smiled, and so did Father Francis Gonzalez, who stood attentively beside them wearing the habit of the Mercedarian Order. Then the Archbishop prayed in Latin, while Father Francis went over to a table and brought back a little dish filled with olive oil and balsam. Rose knew about the dish of oil. It had been blessed the previous Holy Thursday and was to be used in administering the Sacrament of Confirmation. It was called Chrism.

Carts rolled by in the cobblestone streets outside the church. Peddlers shouted their wares and Indian children laughed and played games. But inside it was a different story. Archbishop Turribius, sitting before the high altar, prayed aloud:

> Fill them with the spirit of Thy Fear, and sign them with the Sign of the Cross of Christ, in Thy mercy, unto life eternal. Through the same Jesus Christ Thy Son, Our Lord, Who liveth and reigneth with Thee in the unity of the same Holy Ghost, God, world without end.

Then he dipped the tip of his right thumb into the Chrism and made the Sign of the Cross on the forehead of one little boy, then of the other. Rose lifted her head as the Archbishop came to her. The Holy Ghost was at hand. He would bring her strength and courage to be a really good Christian.

Rose, I sign thee with the Sign of the Cross. And I confirm thee with the Chrism of salvation. In the Name of the Father, and of the Son, and of the Holy Ghost. Amen.

It was over. The child lifted her eyes to the kindly face of the Archbishop. "Peace be with thee," he whispered, and gave her a light tap on the cheek.

CHAPTER 3

THE SECRET

T HERE WAS a great deal of happiness in Rose's heart when she finally left the church. At last she was a soldier of Jesus Christ! From now on she could grow up with the help of four wonderful Sacraments.

"And my name really is Rose now, Mother?"

Maria de Oliva smiled. "That's right," she said. "The good Archbishop gave it to you himself."

So she wouldn't be called Isabel anymore! Rose smiled and took her mother's hand. What a wonderful place the world was! How good it was to be alive, with all Three Persons of the Most Blessed Trinity in one's soul! Then, quite suddenly, the smile faded from the girl's face. Below her, in the great, open Plaza of Quivi, dozens of brightly dressed Indians were gathering menacingly and calling out names.

"Look at the Christians!" they shouted. "They think their God is in the church!"

"Christians! Christians!" jeered the others. "Such fools!"

Rose stared in amazement. Could it be possible that these people were making fun of her?

"Are they talking about us, Mother?"

Maria nodded. "Wretched pagans! They don't know any better. Come along, Rose, before they start any real trouble. Upon my word, such a thing would never happen in Lima! At least we have some law and order there."

Mother and daughter went quickly down the church steps, but before they could reach the bottom a great roar went up from the crowd. Archbishop Turribius had come to the open door of the church and now stood looking down at the people in the Plaza. His face was pale and sad.

"My children, why do you act this way?" he cried sorrowfully. "Haven't you heard that only Christians worship the true God? That He is waiting for you now, here in this church? That He will make your souls as white and clean as the snow on the Andes?"

"Bah!" shrieked an old man. "You're a Spaniard! A big-nosed Spaniard! We don't like you! Go away from our town!"

"Big-nosed Spaniard!" sang a group of children, and the mob took up the cry: "Big-nosed Spaniard! Go away from our town!"

Rose could hardly believe her ears. The whole Plaza was now filling with Indians, laughing and making fun of the good Archbishop. One woman took her market basket and put it on her head as though it were a mitre. Immediately those around bowed to the ground and made the Sign of the Cross as she pretended to bless them.

"ARE THEY TALKING ABOUT US, MOTHER?"

Standing on the church steps, Archbishop Turribius watched the hubbub in silence. Father Francis, who had followed him outside, shook his head.

"I've tried so hard to convert them, Your Excellency. Alas, what is to be done? Quivi is only one little town in these mountains. There are dozens of others, all filled with Indians who insist that their god is the sun. They make golden images of the sun and worship them day and night."

The Archbishop nodded. His face was suddenly stern, and Rose trembled as she saw him advance down the steps toward the jeering throng. His hand was not raised in the usual blessing. Instead, it pointed to Heaven in a terrifying way.

"Disgraceful ones!" cried the Archbishop. "No more than three years will your town be spared from destruction. No longer than that will you live to insult the servants of God!"

"Ha, ha!" cried the people, joining in a circle to dance about the Archbishop. "Our god is the sun," they chanted; "our holy city is Cuzco. You Spaniards have stolen our gold and silver. We have no faith in what you tell us."

Rose and her mother made their way fearfully around the edge of the crowd in the Plaza and entered the street leading to their house. They could still hear the shouts and insults of the Indians, but the mocking faces were gone. There was only the memory of the scene, and of the frightening words the Archbishop had spoken.

As the weeks passed, Rose thought often about

her Confirmation day. Little by little her heart was filling with an urge to do something for the ignorant souls of the Indians. But what? She was only eleven years old, and a girl. Ferdinand had been right. Men and boys could go out into the world and be useful, but what did the future hold for a Peruvian girl? Marriage, maybe. Or the religious life.

"I don't want either of them," thought Rose.

One day an idea came to her. Probably it had been in the back of her mind ever since she had been very young, but the problem of the pagan Indians had brought it into the open.

"If I can't do great deeds, I can try to do little ones well," she told herself. "I can be patient about little troubles, and offer them to God the Father in union with those His Son had in this world. That way they will have merit, and perhaps I can even save a soul or two."

This was a wonderful idea. As Rose grew older, she never forgot it. If she cut her finger for instance, she wouldn't make a fuss about it. A cut finger had little importance in itself, but it could mean a great deal if she offered the pain to God.

"I'll give Him all my happiness, too," she thought. "I'll give Him everything."

So the days passed. Rose didn't tell anyone of her secret, but Ferdinand, who was the closest to her of all her brothers and sisters, suspected something.

"What makes you so happy?" he asked curiously. "Is it because you like living in Quivi, Rose? Is that why you're always singing when you think no one hears you?"

Color flooded the girl's face. "Maybe," she smiled.

Ferdinand looked at his sister sharply and started to whittle a piece of wood. "If you like Quivi so much, perhaps I'd better not spoil things. Last night, though, after Father got home from the mine, I heard something. Can you guess what?"

Rose sat very still. Here was a chance to offer yet another small sacrifice to God. Unsatisfied curiosity was a little thing in itself, but when it was added to the sufferings of Jesus it suddenly took on great value. It could help some unknown sinner; it could release a soul from Purgatory.

Ferdinand stopped carving his piece of wood. "What's the matter with you?" he asked sharply. "You've got the funniest look on your face, Rose, just as though you were praying. Aren't you interested in what Father said?"

Rose smiled. "Of course I'm interested. I'm sorry if you think I wasn't paying attention."

"Oh, it's all right. I just wanted to tell you we're going back to Lima soon. The whole lot of us."

"Back to Lima?"

"Yes. Father doesn't like it at the silver mine. He says a lot of Indians die there every day because they have to work too hard. Worse than that, some of the children are starving because the mine owners won't give the people enough food. Things are going from bad to worse. Those were Father's own words."

Tears came into the girl's eyes. "But it shouldn't be like that, Ferdinand! Peru really belongs to the

Indians, not to the Spaniards. You'd think that after taking away so much gold and silver. . . ."

The boy frowned thoughtfully. "I know. But that doesn't seem to make much difference. I tell you, Rose, we should be awfully glad we're not Indians or Negroes. They just don't have a chance. Did you ever think of that?"

Rose had thought about that very thing many times, but after the family returned to Lima, she pondered it even more. The Indians and Negroes in the city streets there were poor and ragged. Their children had no schooling. There was so much misery for these poor people.

"Can't we do something?" she often thought. "Lord, isn't there some way I could help?"

But no matter how much she prayed, the eleven-year-old girl could think of no material way to help the thousands of wretched Indians and Negroes. She could only continue to offer small sacrifices to God the Father, uniting them to the sufferings of Christ on earth and asking that He bless the natives in their poverty and ignorance.

One morning shortly after her return to Lima, Rose was in the garden behind her father's house. Recently she had received her parents' permission to raise flowers for sale in the public market. It brought in a little money, her mother said, and the work was not too hard. Rose had remarkable skill with plants and flowers, and Gaspar's garden was flourishing as never before.

"Well," said a sudden voice, "is this busy young lady Rose Flores?"

The girl looked up from the clumps of violets she had been setting out and scrambled to her feet. "Doctor John! Why, how nice to see you!"

Doctor John Pérez de Zumeta set down the large package he was carrying. "Your mother said I'd find you out here. And how is my little friend after her trip to Quivi?"

"Very well, thank you, Doctor."

"You're sure of that?"

Rose laughed gaily. "Oh, quite sure. Did you know I'm in business now, Doctor? The flower business? Yesterday some of my roses sold for a very good price at the market."

Doctor John smiled and sat down on a small stone bench. "I heard that good news from Marianna. But it's not about business that I came to see you, Rose. Your mother sent me out here to have a talk with you. It seems she's a bit worried."

Rose's dark eyes widened. "*Worried?* About me? But what have I done, Doctor John? I can't imagine. . . ."

"She tells me you don't eat enough to keep a bird alive. More than that, you don't get your proper sleep because every night, when you think no one is watching you, you get up out of bed to pray."

Rose blushed. "I—I'm sorry," she said. "I didn't think anyone knew about those things."

Doctor John looked down at the girl before him. "You have some kind of secret, haven't you?" he said kindly. "Don't you want to tell me about it? You know you can trust me. Haven't I been your friend ever since you were a baby?"

Rose nodded. "You're so good," she said slowly. "Maybe you will understand."

So the man and child sat together in the big garden. Butterflies of many colors fluttered in the sunshine, and in the thick branches of the olive trees Ferdinand's pet doves murmured gently.

"Well," said Doctor John, "suppose you tell me what it is."

Rose took a deep breath. "I just want to save souls," she said. "Hundreds and hundreds of souls. The only way I know is by prayer and suffering. Isn't that all right, Doctor John?"

CHAPTER 4

ANOTHER VISITOR

DOCTOR JOHN listened to his young friend with interest, but there was nothing she could say that would change his mind. Saving souls was a very fine work indeed, but little girls of eleven needed plenty of food—and at least ten hours of sleep each night.

"You remind me of someone I met just recently," said Doctor John. "The boy is older than you—about eighteen, I imagine. But he has almost the same idea. He wants to save the souls of sinners—Indians, Negroes, white people, everybody."

Rose's dark eyes widened. "A boy?" she asked: "I don't know him, do I?"

Doctor John shook his head. "Probably not. His name is Martin de Porres. Right now his father is Governor of Panama, but his mother is just a poor Negro woman. She lives with Doña Francisca Vélez over near the Church of San Lázaro."

Rose said nothing. Martin de Porres! She had heard that name somewhere. Hadn't one of the priests from the Dominican church?...

"Martin used to be an assistant to my old friend, Doctor Marcelo de Rivero," Doctor John continued. "These last three years, however, he's been helping the Dominican priests at their monastery. He's not a lay Brother, just a simple Tertiary helper. And pretty capable, too, from all accounts."

Rose nodded. "I hope he saves lots of souls," she said softly. "Doctor John, the world needs so many prayers! If you had seen those poor pagan Indians in Quivi..."

The man got up from the stone bench. "Those Indians must have made a deep impression on you, child. But you can't be thinking about them all the time. Here—I brought you a little present. It ought to come in handy one of these days."

The present turned out to be the large package which Doctor John had brought with him into the garden. Rose watched eagerly as he undid the wrappings.

"It's a little rose bush!" she cried. "Oh, Doctor John! Is it a white one? I mean, will it have white flowers?"

The doctor smiled. "So I was told. A friend brought it to me yesterday from his country place at Limatambo. I thought you might like to have it, seeing you're now in the flower business."

Rose beamed with joy. Doctor John was really the nicest man! He had always been a good friend of hers, even on that dreadful day when he had cut out her thumb nail because it had become diseased. She had been only three years old then, but the memory of the sharp knife was still fresh.

"IT'S A LITTLE ROSE BUSH!" SHE CRIED.

"A white rose bush was just what I wanted," she said happily. "Marianna says the rich ladies always ask their servants to pick out white roses at the market. Thank you so much, Doctor John."

The man smiled. "You're welcome, child. And now all I want from you is the promise to take care of your health. Will you give it to me? Will you stop thinking so much about sinners and look after yourself properly?"

Rose laughed. "I won't get sick, Doctor John. Now that I'm in charge of this garden, there isn't time to be sick. Besides the flowers, I have the vegetables and herbs to tend, and the fruit trees, too. It's quite a bit of work. But I'm so happy, Doctor John! At last I've found a way to be useful to the family."

Yet when she was once more alone, Rose sighed wearily. So Mother was worried about her—Mother thought she spent too much time praying!

"It isn't so," the girl told herself. "No one could pray too much."

As she sat there on the bench, with the sun flooding the garden and the doves cooing above her head, a little sadness crept into Rose's heart. If only someone in the family understood! But there was no one who cared very much about saving souls.

More than that: though nothing had been said recently, Rose knew that the money which came in from the flower sales was only enough to pay a very few bills. In five or six years, therefore, she would be expected to do more than raise fruit and flowers to sell in Lima's public market: she would

be expected to marry a Spaniard with a good name
and a good fortune. There were many such in the
city now—boys whose fathers had come out from
Spain to find wealth in the mines of the Andes.

A black and white butterfly fluttered gently to
the rose bush at her feet, and Rose forgot about
her troubles. Such a lovely creature, this black and
white butterfly, with its wings glowing like velvet
in the bright sunshine.

"Maybe some day I can wear black and white,
too," she thought. "That boy Doctor John told me
about—Martin de Porres. He must wear it if he
lives in the Dominican monastery."

But a girl couldn't live at Santo Domingo—only
Dominican priests and lay Brothers, and Tertiary
helpers like Martin—and there was no Dominican
convent for women in Lima.

"Besides, I don't think God wants me to be a
nun," thought Rose. "I think He just wants me to
live here at home and save souls by prayer."

The silence in the garden was suddenly broken.
Marianna was hurrying down the path, her red sandals crunching on the gravel.

"Miss Rose! Your mother wants you to come in
the house at once. Someone's here to see you."

A chill settled on the girl's heart. Hardly a day
passed that ladies did not come calling on Maria
de Oliva. Always Rose was expected to be there, to
play her guitar, to sing songs, to be useful in enter-
taining the guests. This would not be so bad if only
the ladies were sensible like Doctor John. But they
chattered and gossiped about the most foolish

things. And sometimes they were very unkind about ladies who were not present.

"I was just going to plant this rose bush, Marianna. But I'll come right away—if Mother really needs me."

The Indian girl, guessing her thoughts, laughed. "Don't feel too bad. The lady with your Mother is Doña Maria de Quiñones."

"*Doña Maria!*"

"That's right. It's been quite a while since she was here."

Rose's dark eyes brightened. Oh, this was different! Doña Maria, the niece of Archbishop Turribius, was a lovely person. Although she had a beautiful home and many servants, Doña Maria was very humble. And every day, in spite of all her social duties, she managed to pay a visit to Our Lord in the Blessed Sacrament.

"I'm glad she's the one," Rose said simply. "I'll come right away, Marianna. Only first I'll have to clean up a little. My hands are dirty from planting the violets."

Marianna nodded. "Be sure to wear your new blue dress," she cautioned. "And before you go in to see Doña Maria, come down to the kitchen. I have a pretty red flower for your hair."

Presently Rose entered the front parlor of her father's house. Her long dark hair had been neatly brushed, and fastened at the side was a red poppy. The blue silk dress was of the latest style for young girls; it had a full skirt and a narrow silver belt that had come from the famous mining city of Potosí.

On her feet were sandals trimmed with white llama fur.

Maria de Oliva beamed with pride as Rose came into the room. "Well, here she is at last, Doña Maria. How do you think she looks?"

Doña Maria de Quiñones smiled and held out both her arms. "My dear, I think she looks wonderful!"

Rose moved quickly across the room to the big chair by the window where Doña Maria was sitting. The lady was dressed in grey silk, and a black lace veil was draped softly over her hair. On her fingers glistened a number of rings, while from her throat hung a fine golden chain with a little cross of diamonds on the end. Rose sat down on a stool near the visitor's feet.

"I'm so glad you came," she said simply, looking up into the kindly face above her.

Maria de Oliva nodded. "Doña Maria has only a few minutes to spare us today, Rose. She's on her way to the seminary with some food for the students."

"Yes. Would you like to come with me, dear?"

The girl nodded eagerly. She knew about the seminary, although she had never been there. Archbishop Turribius had founded it not so long ago for young men who wanted to be secular priests. Apart from the different monasteries, such as those of Saint Francis and Saint Dominic, there had been no seminary in all South America for students for the priesthood.

"I'd love to go with you, Doña Maria. May I, Mother?"

"Of course, child. Only first play a little something on your guitar for Doña Maria. It's been a long time since she heard you. And while you're doing that, I'll go and see if there isn't a cake I could send over to the seminary."

The guitar was hanging in its usual place on the wall. Rose took it down and tuned the strings. "I made up a little song the other day," she told the visitor shyly. "It's nothing much."

Doña Maria nodded. "Let me hear it. I've always liked your songs, Rose."

The girl sat down with the guitar across her lap, and began to sing.

> *Dearest Lord,*
> *How good to see*
> *Your beauty in the flowers*
> *And the green olive tree!*
> *How good to know*
> *You wait to bless*
> *My little heart*
> *With happiness!*

Doña Maria smiled. What a lovely child this was, and how unspoiled! No wonder people predicted a great future for her. It would be hard to find a prettier or more gifted young girl in all Peru.

"It's not only that she's clever," Doña Maria thought. "There's something that sets this child apart. I can see it in her eyes. I just wonder what she'll do with her life."

Presently Rose's slim fingers played a final chord.

"That's all," she told her visitor. "It's just a little bit of a song, like all the others."

"A little prayer, maybe?"

"I like to think so, Doña Maria."

It was quiet in the big front parlor. The woman looked at the girl tenderly. "You think a lot about Our Lord, don't you, Rose?"

"Yes." She spoke hardly above a whisper. "He's always interested in us, whether we're young or old, rich or poor. If we try to be good, He's always in our hearts. Dear Doña Maria, the only time I'm really happy is when I remember to think of Him deep in my heart, helping me to come to Him in Heaven!"

CHAPTER 5

TWO STORIES

THE VISIT to the seminary was interesting, but Doña Maria de Quiñones did not stay long. She informed Rose that she had other places to visit.

"The nuns at the Monastery of the Incarnation?"

"That's right. Afterward perhaps we'll have time to go to the Monastery of the Conception. And to the Trinity, too."

Doña Maria's carriage rolled swiftly through the narrow streets. Rose followed the busy scenes about her with interest, although it was not the magnificent buildings or the many colorful gardens which chiefly claimed her attention. Instead, it was the people in the streets—cripples and beggars and ragged little children. There were so many of them! And they seemed to have forgotten how to smile!

Doña Maria threw a swift glance at her young companion. "I can guess what you're thinking, my dear."

The girl's dark eyes shone. "I was thinking that if I were a boy, I'd go to Santo Domingo tomorrow so I could be a priest and do something for all these poor people. So many of them don't know a thing about God, Doña Maria. And there aren't enough priests here in Peru to teach them. It's a pity, isn't it?"

The woman nodded. "A great pity, child. But tell me why you'd like to be a Dominican. Why not a Franciscan, or a Jesuit, or an Augustinian?"

Rose smiled. So many other people were always asking the same question. "Because of Saint Catherine of Siena, Doña Maria. She was a Dominican Tertiary. And such a wonderful person! We have a book at home that tells about her. I've read it so many times that I must know every word by now."

"I've read about her, too. She certainly *was* a wonderful person. But she was a Tertiary, spending all her days in the world. She never entered a convent."

"I know, Doña Maria. She belonged to the Third Order of Saint Dominic. It must be a lovely life, since she loved it so much."

"And a hard life, child. It takes a very special grace to become a saint while you go on living in the world."

Rose laughed. "I'm going to try, Doña Maria. I won't ever marry or enter a convent. I've asked Saint Catherine to help me be like her. You see, when I was just five years old . . ."

"Yes?"

"It sounds like a rather foolish story, for I was very small then."

Doña Maria smiled. "You tell me your story and

then I'll tell one," she said. "By that time we should have reached the Monastery of the Incarnation. But of course if you want to keep it a secret. . ."

Rose shook her head. "It's not that important. Besides, when I'm older and people expect me to marry, I'll have to explain why I can't. So I'll tell you first. I know you'll understand."

"Thank you, my dear. I'll respect your confidence."

"It was one afternoon when Ferdinand and I were playing in the garden," began Rose. "I was five and he was seven. Marianna had just washed my hair and I was pleased with the way it shone in the sun. It was soft and silky and it had little curls in it. I was proud of those curls, Doña Maria."

"No doubt they were nice."

"But Ferdinand began to make fun of me. He pretended he was a priest preaching a sermon, and he talked about how foolish it is to be proud of one's clothes and one's looks. He said people go to Hell for things like that. As I sat there listening to him, he suddenly took up a handful of dirt and threw it over my clean hair.

"'You needn't be proud any more,' he said.

"At first I was really cross with Ferdinand. But after I thought it over I decided he was right. We really shouldn't be so concerned over our looks, or whether we have money or health or education. Of course he was only playing a game. He never thought I'd take him seriously. But I did. Then everyone was terribly angry with me."

"Why, child?"

"Because I decided to cut off my curls, as Saint Catherine of Siena did when she was a little girl; then I wouldn't be proud of my looks any more."

Doña Maria laughed. "Your mother never told me about that," she said. "And I'm glad your hair has grown again, Rose. It's really very pretty."

"Thank you, Doña Maria. Only there's more to my story than that. You see, when I cut off my hair, I promised Our Lord that I would always love Him more than anyone or anything. I was only five, but I knew that all I wanted in life was to serve Him and to work for His glory here on earth. I didn't want a husband or a home or children—only Him."

"I understand."

"Of course Mother doesn't know about this, and probably she'll be angry when I do tell her. But that's the way it is, Doña Maria. And there's nothing anyone can do that will make me change my mind. I belong to God—forever and ever!"

Doña Maria smiled. "That's a lovely story," she said softly. "And I'm sure it will have a splendid ending some day. But don't be surprised if it's a bit different from the one you plan."

"Different?"

"Yes. When you grow older you may find your vocation is to be a nun, not a Dominican Tertiary like Saint Catherine. After all, considering the gifts God has given you, it may be wiser to serve Him in the religious life than in the world."

"Maybe, Doña Maria. But right now I don't think so."

The woman smiled. "Well, we'll see. Now suppose

I tell you my story. We've almost come to the Monastery of the Incarnation and I want you to hear it before we get there."

"Oh yes, Doña Maria. I'd nearly forgotten that you have a story, too."

The woman settled back in the carriage. "It was on January 6, 1535, that Don Francisco Pizarro founded our city of Lima. You know that as well as I do, Rose. And you know, too, how he was murdered by his enemies in 1541. Well, for some years afterward things were unsettled in Peru. Some of Pizarro's followers wanted to rule the country themselves, and they urged people to revolt against the lawful ruler, the King of Spain. One of these rebels was Captain Francisco Hernández de Girón. He was finally caught, however, and executed on December 9, 1554. His body was then put in a sack and tied to a horse to be dragged through the streets of Lima."

"What a dreadful thing to do!"

"Yes. It was meant to be a warning to others who might revolt against the King of Spain. However, the one who suffered most through all this was the Captain's wife, Doña Mencia. She saw the whole dreadful punishment—even her husband's body being dragged through the streets. For weeks she could not get rid of the memory. Finally she told her mother, Doña Leonor Portocarrero, that she wanted to spend the rest of her days praying for Captain Francisco's soul. Even though he had died as a common criminal, perhaps God's mercy had saved him from Hell. Perhaps he was even then in

Purgatory, suffering for his sins and crying out for
prayers from his friends."

"So what did she do, Doña Maria?"

"Doña Leonor agreed with Doña Mencia; she,
too, had wished to devote her life to prayer. So they
visited Father Andrew, the Prior of the Augustinian
monastery near their home. They told him about
the unfortunate Captain, and explained that they
wanted to be nuns and spend the rest of their days
praying for his soul."

Rose smiled. "He let them do it, Doña Maria?
He helped them build the first convent for women
in Lima?"

Doña Maria stared at her companion. "You know
this story as well as I do, Rose! Why didn't you tell
me?"

"Because I love to hear you talk. You make things
so interesting. Really, though, I didn't know the
whole story. Not the part about the poor Captain's
body being dragged through the streets."

"Well, it's true. And it's also true that Doña
Leonor and Doña Mencia received the Augustinian
habit from Father Andrew and started to lead the
religious life in their own house. That was around
1558. Some people didn't approve of the idea at all.
They thought the two women should have waited
until they had more money and more helpers. But
there was the Captain's soul to remember, you see."

"They didn't have to wait too long to have a real
monastery, did they?"

"Only three years. There it is down the street,
child—the Monastery of the Incarnation. It was

ROSE CARRIED THE BASKET OF FOOD
DOÑA MARIA HAD BROUGHT FOR THE NUNS.

built in 1561."

The towers of the monastery were before them, and the thick adobe wall that shut off the garden from the street. Rose turned to her companion eagerly as the carriage drove up to the front door.

"Lima has been first in so many things, Doña Maria. Father was telling us just the other day that we have the first university in all America. It was founded in the Dominican convent on May 12, 1551, by Father Thomas of San Martin."

"Aha, you do like the Dominicans, Rose! You're always singing their praises."

"But it's true, Doña Maria. The University of San Marcos was first."

"Don't forget the seminary we just visited. It's a pioneer venture, too. And we have the first hospital—Santa Ana."

"Founded by a Dominican, Doña Maria, in 1549. You've not forgotten that our first Archbishop, Jerome de Loaysa, belonged to Saint Dominic's family?"

The woman threw up her hands in mock despair. "Come along, child! You know more than I do about Lima's history."

Rose found the basket of food which Doña Maria had brought for the nuns. As she followed her friend toward the heavy wooden gate, she had a sudden wonderful idea. Maybe Lima would be first in something else—the first place in all the Americas to have a canonized saint!

"Perhaps Doña Maria's own uncle, Archbishop Turribius," she thought. "He's such a holy man!"

CHAPTER 6

A SAINT COMES TO LIMA

TIME PASSED. On the afternoon of August 23, 1601—the vigil of the feast of Saint Bartholomew—Marianna, the Indian servant woman, hummed a happy little tune as she turned into the street of Santo Domingo. Early that morning she had left Gaspar's house with two large baskets of flowers. Now the baskets were empty, and there was a jingle of many silver coins in her purse. It had been an exceptionally fine day at the market. Every one of the flowers had sold for a good price.

"I guess there's no one like Miss Rose when it comes to raising flowers," she thought. "Her mother will be so pleased at the way things went today."

But when Marianna opened the back door of the big house there was no sign of Maria de Oliva or of the children. No one was at home to whom she could tell the good news.

"I remember now," she thought. "The whole family has gone to the Franciscan church. That new priest, Father Francis Solano, is preaching there today. Already they call the good man 'Saint Francis' because of the many wonderful things he's done."

Marianna took off her big straw hat and went into the kitchen. In a few minutes she would have to start getting supper. Already the sunlight was beginning to fade—such sunlight as there was, for in Lima during August there were few sunny days. In this respect the city was not at all like Arequipa and Cuzco, those other Peruvian towns high in the Andes. Generally, during August, it was damp and foggy along the coast, while in the mountains the sun shone most of the day.

"I'll build a fire in a minute and that will help take off the evening chill," Marianna told herself. "As for this money, I'd better hide it in a safe place. It's the most Miss Rose's flowers ever brought."

While Marianna was putting away the silver coins she heard a melodious sound. Someone was singing at the back of the garden, and mingled with the sweet notes was the rippling call of a nightingale. Marianna pushed the money out of sight and tiptoed to the door. The words of the song were distinct:

> *You sing to your Maker,*
> *To a Lover, I;*
> *Both of us delight in*
> *Praising the Most High.*

"So Miss Rose has been here all the time!" thought Marianna. I might have guessed it. All her free time she spends in that little shrine she built!"

It did not take long to start a fire on the big open hearth. Marianna made a hurried trip to the well near the back door, then set a kettle of water on to boil. Rose was still singing, accompanied by the nightingale, when she finally started down the gravel path to the back of the garden. The sky was darkening now, and a little wind moved through the branches of the tall trees. Marianna shivered.

"Miss Rose! It's time to get supper ready!"

There was no answer. The Indian woman sighed and started to pick her way through the rapidly falling darkness. The Flores garden with its many shrubs and flowers was a pleasant enough place in the daytime, but at night it was a different story. The great drooping branches of the banana trees seemed weird and threatening. The olive and fig trees loomed up dark and strange. Often Maria de Oliva had complained that the garden was no safe place at night.

Rose, however, was not afraid of the dark. Three years before, when she had been only twelve years old, she had built herself a little oratory in a spot as far away from the house as possible. It was really a sort of hut made of bent twigs and branches; inside she had a small altar, with a crucifix and candles. The little shrine was a good place, she had told the family, in which to work and pray.

"Most fifteen-year-old girls," thought Marianna, "are anxious about having a good time, but not Miss Rose. It's still souls that are her great concern. How to save them from Hell, how to make herself more pleasing to God—those are the things she thinks about."

It was damp as well as dark where Marianna finally stopped. There, hidden among the banana trees, she could make out Rose's little oratory. Overhead the nightingale still uttered an occasional note. Marianna pushed aside a spreading branch.

"Miss Rose! Don't you know you'll catch your death of cold staying in this damp place? Why can't you say your prayers somewhere else?"

From the darkness of the little hermitage Rose laughed. It was a warm and mellow sound, and instantly Marianna was sorry she had spoken so harshly.

"I'm all right, Marianna. The little bird and I. . ."

"I heard you. But it's time for supper, child. You'd better save your singing for tomorrow."

Rose came out of the tiny shelter. "I guess it is growing chilly, Marianna. I didn't notice before, though, because I was so busy all afternoon. First I did some sewing. Then, when it got too dark, the bird came. . ."

Marianna peered into the oratory. A wooden cross was standing against the wall. It was as tall as Rose herself. A shudder ran through the Indian woman as she realized that Rose had been doing other things besides sewing and singing hymns. Sometime during the afternoon she had carried that heavy cross around the garden, in remembrance of Our Lord's painful journey to Calvary. It was a practice she had had for some years—a very special method of making the Way of the Cross when she was alone.

"WHY CAN'T YOU SAY YOUR PRAYERS
SOMEWHERE ELSE?"

The woman thrust away the thought impatiently. "Come along, Miss Rose. I'll need some help with the supper."

The girl nodded and picked up a large piece of linen. It was an altar cloth which Maria de Oliva had asked her to hem. She had finished the task earlier in the afternoon.

As the two walked toward the house, Rose observed someone moving about in the kitchen, near the window.

"Mother must be home from church," she told her companion.

"I wouldn't be surprised, Miss Rose. She's been gone a long time. Probably Father Francis preached another of his fine sermons."

"He must be wonderful!"

"We'll soon find out. But don't run like that! You might trip on a stone."

Rose smiled. The darkness that had now settled over the garden meant little to her. She knew every inch of the place. But she slowed her steps, nevertheless. It was hardly kind to let Marianna find her way through the gloom alone.

"I'd have loved to go to church this afternoon, Marianna. Everyone in Lima talks about how holy Father Francis is. He's been a missionary for eleven years. And they say he's converted thousands of Indians."

"Then why didn't you go to hear him?"

"I had to hem this altar cloth for Mother."

"You know that could have waited, child. Your mother would have been only too glad..."

"I wanted to make a little sacrifice."

"*Sacrifice!* Miss Rose, if I hear that word again . . ."

"Please don't be cross, Marianna. I love to make sacrifices. It's my way of being useful to people. Sometimes I think that's why I was born—so I could pray and suffer for others."

"If you make too many sacrifices, you won't be long in this world."

Rose smiled. "I don't mind. I know I'll be here as long as God wishes. And now, Marianna, I'll tell you a secret."

"What?"

"Tomorrow is the feast of Saint Bartholomew."

"That's no secret."

"No, but this is. When I come to die, I think it will be on Saint Bartholomew's feast. Every year, when August 24 comes around, I get so excited. Oh, Marianna, it must be wonderful to live in Heaven and see God all the time!"

"Miss Rose! You musn't say such things!"

"And why not? Some people look forward to their birthdays, but to me it's more sensible to look forward to the day you die. That's really a great day, Marianna—the day real living begins."

The Indian woman made a large Sign of the Cross. "Don't let your mother hear this nonsense about dying on Saint Bartholomew's day. She wouldn't like it at all, Miss Rose. Besides, it's wrong to let people think you know about the future. That's God's business."

Rose nodded. "It was He who told me," she said simply.

It was true. Often, in the depths of her soul, Rose heard wonderful things. Sometimes it was Our Lord who spoke to her. Other times it was the Blessed Virgin. Or Saint Catherine of Siena. Always they made her understand that men and women must do penance for their sins. For a soul with even the tiniest stain upon it can never enter Heaven. Either the sinner makes up for that sin himself, in Purgatory or in this world, or someone else does so for him: and that was what Rose meant by being useful to people.

"I want to make up for people's sins," she would say; "Lord, just tell me what You wish me to do."

As Marianna and her young companion reached the back door, they stopped suddenly. Over the high adobe wall that shut off the Flores garden from the street had come the heartrending cry of a woman in pain. Rose peered into the darkness.

"Someone must be hurt, Marianna. That cry came from just outside the gate."

"Mother of God, child, don't go to see what's wrong! There's no telling what may be the trouble."

"But we can't stay here and not help her!"

As Rose started running down the path, another scream pierced the night air. Hearing the commotion, Maria de Oliva opened the kitchen window. "What's going on out there, Marianna? Why aren't you getting supper ready?"

The Indian woman twisted her hands nervously. "Miss Rose has gone out to the street, *señora.* She—she thinks someone is in trouble."

"Gone out to the street? At this hour?"

Just then the wooden gate clicked open and slow footsteps could be heard on the gravel path. "It's all right, Mother. This poor woman fell and hurt her knee on the walk."

Maria de Oliva leaned out the window. What she saw made her gasp. Rose was coming slowly toward the house, an old Indian woman leaning on her shoulder.

"She's half starved as well as hurt, Mother. And she's cold, too."

Maria de Oliva stared helplessly into the darkened garden. Most of the Indians in Lima were dirty. Some were diseased. Rose was not only touching one of them, she was apparently going to bring her into the house. The Indian woman was hurt—well, let her go to the Hospital of Santa Ana on the other side of town. Jerome de Loaysa, the first Archbishop, had made it accessible to every sick Indian in Lima.

Maria was almost overcome with anxiety and anger. Something else, however, was also stirring within her, and for once in her life she found herself without words. Just an hour ago she had been listening to the sermon of a Franciscan friar. The sermon had been on charity. Father Francis Solano, fresh from his missionary labors in Paraguay and Argentina, had not spared his listeners. He had had no soft words for the selfish.

"You either love your neighbor or you do not," he had said. "You either see Christ in him or your own pride. And what you see determines whether you go to Heaven or to Hell. Oh, my brothers!

Never turn away from a man because he is poor, because he is ignorant, because his skin is another color from yours! Remember, you may be turning away from God!"

Maria de Oliva left the window to open the kitchen door. "Bring the woman in," she muttered lamely. "At least we can give her a good meal."

CHAPTER 7

A FRIEND IN NEED

AS ROSE grew older, she obtained her father's permission to care for many other poor women who were ill. A special room was set aside for these unfortunates. It was known as "The Infirmary," and very rapidly became a real haven for Lima's sick poor.

Rose's heart was full of love for these sufferers because her heart was full of love for God. To be good to the sick was to love Our Lord. No matter how sickening a disease might be, Rose did not refuse to help anyone. Sometimes a really terrible infected wound would be too much for her stomach to bear, and she would have to leave and go outside for a few minutes. Then, after pulling herself together, she would return to her patient with a kind smile on her face.

As the months passed, several Indians reported that they had been cured of their ailments at "The Infirmary," especially after Rose had let them hold her little statue of the Child Jesus. This statue, they insisted, was miraculous. Rose herself referred to it as "The Little Doctor."

Despite her daughter's popularity with the poor of Lima, Maria de Oliva sometimes lost her temper over the number of cases in "The Infirmary."

"Aren't there enough hospitals in Lima without turning our house into one?" she demanded of her husband one day. "Santa Ana, San Andrés, San Lázaro—really, there's no reason why Rose should keep so many wretched women here, Gaspar. It makes me sick!"

Gaspar Flores smiled. Hardly a day passed that his energetic wife did not complain about something.

"We have a big house, Maria. Surely Rose can use one room for her charity."

"*Charity!* Gaspar, do you realize this is the year 1606? Rose is twenty years old and not married yet! Surely I have a right to complain when she spends hours at a time with sick Indians and Negroes. Why can't she be interested in meeting some nice young men for a change?"

"What good would that be? You know what the child told us."

A shadow crossed Maria's face. So Gaspar really believed that his daughter could never marry because she had promised herself to God at the age of five. What nonsense! No child of five understood about such things.

"If Rose doesn't marry, I'll die of shame!" she declared flatly. "Already people are starting to talk. They say there's something wrong with her mind, that she's strange. . ."

Gaspar sighed. Rose had always been different from his other children. Even when she was very small there were things about her that puzzled him. The stories she told, for instance. Was it really possible that the Child Jesus had taught her to read and write? That she saw her Guardian Angel? That the Blessed Mother often appeared to her as she worked in the garden?

"Maybe it's God's Will that Rose enter a convent," he said presently. "We owe at least one of our eleven children to the religious life, Maria. Rose is well suited, it seems to me. . ."

"That girl enters a convent over my dead body," proclaimed his wife grimly. "For years I've placed all my hopes on her marrying well. Do you think I'm going to be disappointed now?"

What, Gaspar thought, was the use of arguing? During the twenty-nine years of their married life, Maria had always had her own way.

There were many in Lima who agreed with Gaspar, however, declaring that Rose had all the qualities necessary for a religious vocation. Eventually these came to include the city's treasurer, Don Gonzalo de Massa.

A native of Burgos, Spain, Don Gonzalo had arrived in Lima in the year 1601. Shortly thereafter he had met the Flores family. Despite his wealth and high rank, he was an exceedingly humble man, and his Negro and Indian servants considered themselves fortunate to work in his house. Didn't Don Gonzalo hear Mass every morning in one of the city's several churches? And hadn't he given orders that no poor person was ever to be sent away hungry from his door? As for his wife, Doña Maria de Usátegui—where was a finer Christian woman to be found?

On the morning when Gaspar and his wife were discussing Rose's future, Don Gonzalo was on his way to hear Mass at the Dominican church. It was the day after Easter, a bright, cheerful morning late in March. As his carriage rolled swiftly through the narrow streets, Don Gonzalo chuckled. The children were waiting for him as usual: ragged urchins who knew he always carried a bag of silver coins just for them. There were shouts of welcome as he approached, and the eager youngsters scrambled toward the carriage.

"God bless you, young friends!" he cried, scattering a shower of silver coins through the air. "Take care the horses don't trample them, John."

"*Sí, señor,*" smiled the Indian driver. But neither he nor the horses needed a reminder to go carefully. They knew what to expect when Don Gonzalo set out for Mass in the morning.

The carriage had almost reached the Dominican church when the great bells of the cathedral suddenly began to sound. Their heavy, solemn notes said that death had come to some important person. Presently other bells joined in the mournful music. From all corners of the city the deep tones boomed out—in strange contrast to the joyful Easter strains of the day before.

Don Gonzalo sat tense in his handsome carriage. "It's my old friend, Father John de Lorenzana, who's dead!" he thought. "Why didn't I go to see him yesterday as I planned? I had plenty of time, even if it was Easter Sunday."

It was too late to mend matters now. As his carriage swung into a side street, Don Gonzalo murmured a brief prayer for the good Dominican priest who had been his confessor. Then his eyes brightened as he saw a familiar figure coming down the street—the holy Negro, Martin de Porres.

Martin had at first been just a simple Tertiary helper at Santo Domingo. Three years before, however, in obedience to his Superiors' demands, he had become a regular lay Brother. The greater part of his twenty-seven years had been spent in ministering to the unfortunates of Lima. It little mattered whether these sufferers were rich or poor—Spaniards, Indians or Negroes. Brother Martin's charity knew no bounds. Not a day passed, moreover, that the wonders worked by his prayers were not experienced by some individual or household in the city.

"God be praised!" said Don Gonzalo. "The very man I want to see! John, let me out here and take the carriage home. I want to talk to Brother Martin."

"*Sí, señor,*" said the Indian with a quick smile.

The lay Brother was walking slowly, his head bowed and his lips moving in prayer. He wore a patched white habit under an old black cloak. On his arm was a basket of food. A small brown dog, tail erect, trotted happily at his heels.

"Wait a minute, Martin!"

The lay Brother looked up.

"Good morning, Your Excellency. May the blessings of this holy Eastertide remain with you forever!"

Don Gonzalo stretched out a nervous hand. "Brother Martin—could it be that these bells are tolling for Father John de Lorenzana? Has the good man gone from us?"

The lay Brother smiled. "I was with Father John this morning. He is no longer ill."

"No longer ill? But that can't be! Last week he was at death's door!"

"He will be out of bed tomorrow."

Don Gonzalo stared. "Then these bells ring for another?"

"Yes, Your Excellency. A message has just come from Saña. Archbishop Turribius died there four days ago."

"No!"

"He passed away Holy Thursday afternoon," said Brother Martin calmly. "Although no messenger could get here until now, many people have already guessed the truth. The nuns at the Monastery of the Incarnation, for instance, saw a bright cross in the sky last Thursday. There was an eclipse of the moon that night, too. The Sisters believe these were signs to show that God had taken the Archbishop to Himself."

By now the continued pealing of the bells had brought hundreds of people into the street. As the news spread that their beloved Archbishop was dead, many of them burst into tears. What would

they do without the kindly man who had been their
spiritual shepherd for twenty-five years—who had
shared with the poor all his worldly goods?

Don Gonzalo sighed. "I was in Callao all last
week, Martin. There was a boat just in from Spain
and I had orders to inspect the cargo. But there's
no excuse for my not knowing about the Archbishop. This morning my daughter Micaela tried to
tell me something about those signs in the sky. May
God forgive me! I was in too much of a hurry to
listen."

Martin smiled. "I think I know why, Your
Excellency. You wanted to hear Mass at the
Dominican church. And now I've made you late."

Don Gonzalo shook his head. "No, Martin.
There's still a little time left. But you—you are
going somewhere with this basket of food?"

The lay Brother nodded. "There's a poor woman
in the next street who's suffering from leprosy.
You'll say a prayer that her health improves?"

Don Gonzalo smiled. Brother Martin had his own
way of going about his works of mercy. He always
asked the prayers of others for his sick friends.
Then, when the latter were suddenly cured, he
attributed the wonder to other people's goodness.
Sometimes he even said it was some new medicine.

"I'll say a prayer, all right," replied Don Gonzalo,
"but you're really not fooling me, Martin. Haven't
we just finished the holy season of Lent? In that
time you must have done enough good deeds to
cure an army of lepers."

Martin shook his head. "Your Excellency, why

make fun of me? I'm only a poor Negro."

"A poor Negro who spends himself for others. God bless you, Brother Martin! And say a prayer for me, too!"

With a hasty handshake for his saintly friend, Don Gonzalo hurried off to the Dominican church. The place was crowded when he arrived, for several Masses were being offered for the repose of the soul of Archbishop Turribius. A young lay Brother led the newcomer to a seat near the Epistle side of the church, close to the Rosary Shrine. Here Father Francis de Vega, the newly-elected Provincial of the Dominicans, was offering Mass.

Don Gonzalo settled himself to assist at the Holy Sacrifice with proper zeal, but presently he suffered a distraction. It was caused by his sudden glimpse of two people a few yards away. The first was a young man of twenty-two, who shifted restlessly from one position to another. The second was a girl of twenty, head and shoulders draped in a black lace veil, her whole being intent upon the actions of the priest at the altar.

"That's Rose Flores," Don Gonzalo told himself. "Wouldn't you know she'd bring Ferdinand to church on such a day as this."

Try as he would, Don Gonzalo found it increasingly difficult to take his thoughts away from the girl before him. How still she knelt, watching Father Francis de Vega offer the Holy Sacrifice! Yet she must be weak; only yesterday his wife had told him that Rose had scarcely tasted any food during the whole of Lent.

"THAT'S ROSE FLORES..."

"She'd be better off in some convent," thought Don Gonzalo. "Probably the only thing that's keeping her out is the fact that her family is poor. They need the money she gets from her flower sales. Besides, Gaspar Flores is probably too poor to supply his daughter with a dowry."

Quite suddenly Don Gonzalo was struck with an idea. Why couldn't he be of help? As a man high in political circles, he had plenty of money and influence. It would be only a small matter to him to see to it that Rose had an adequate dowry and that her family received some honorable kind of help.

"I'll do it!" he told himself. "It will be a real pleasure to help the child." And as he pondered the part he was about to play in this young girl's life, Don Gonzalo felt a great wave of happiness sweep over him.

But, he wondered: When he offered Rose the chance to become a nun, which of Lima's five convents would she choose? Perhaps the newest one, the Franciscan Monastery of Santa Clara, that the good Archbishop (Lord rest his soul!) had founded only two months before.

The more he dwelt upon the idea, the better it seemed. The life of a Poor Clare nun was hard, yet Rose surely knew how to bear suffering. According to his wife, scarcely a day passed that the girl did not have some sacrifice, cheerfully accepted, to offer to God.

"Once she's in a convent she'll be spared at least one trial," thought the man. She won't have to keep avoiding the young men who come to pay her flattering compliments, and her mother won't be able to marry her off to someone who isn't worthy."

Suddenly a little bell tinkled. Don Gonzalo looked toward the altar with a guilty air. "What's the matter with me?" he chided himself. "I haven't been paying attention to this Mass at all!"

CHAPTER 8

FAREWELL TO SANTO DOMINGO

DON GONZALO was not the only one to think it well for Rose to be a Poor Clare. Her old friend, Doña Maria de Quiñones, had had the same idea ever since she had helped her uncle, Archbishop Turribius, establish the Franciscan Monastery of Santa Clara.

"Why don't you want to be a nun?" she asked one day, as the two sat talking in Gaspar's garden. "Think of the peace you would have in the convent! Think of the happiness of giving yourself wholly to God! My dear, Don Gonzalo has told me everything. If it's a matter of the dowry, or what your family will do without the money from your flowers, don't worry another minute. Don Gonzalo will look after everything."

Rose nodded. "He wants me to be a Poor Clare," she said slowly. "And you have the same idea. Oh, Doña Maria, I don't know what to do!"

The woman smiled. She knew what was the trouble. Long ago Rose had given her heart to the Order of Saint Dominic, and as yet there were no

66

Dominican nuns in Lima.

"You're twenty years old now. If you're really sure you don't want to marry..."

"I'm very sure, Doña Maria."

"Then why wait? If God wanted you to be a Dominican, surely He would have seen to it that a convent of those nuns should be here for you."

"Saint Catherine of Siena wasn't a nun. Perhaps I could be a Dominican Tertiary just as she was."

"And live in the world? Put up with all kinds of misunderstandings? Rose, my dear, a long time ago I told you how hard it is to lead a single life in the world. It takes a very special grace. With the love God has given you for prayer and sacrifice—well, I can't help thinking you belong in a convent."

"In Santa Clara?"

"Naturally the Monastery of Santa Clara is very close to my heart. But there are four others in Lima. How would you like to be an Augustinian? The Monastery of the Incarnation is the first convent for women in the New World. It would be a great honor to be accepted there, Rose."

The girl sighed. It really shouldn't matter so much. One could serve God under the Rule of Saint Augustine or of Saint Clare as well as under that of Saint Dominic. Yet why did her whole soul cry out to be a Dominican? Why had she always taken Saint Catherine of Siena for her special model? Even the black and white butterflies in her father's garden—she had always preferred them to any others because they reminded her of the two colors in the Dominican habit.

Weeks passed, and finally Rose confided to Ferdinand that she had made up her mind. If Don Gonzalo was still willing to provide her with a dowry, she would become an Augustinian at the Monastery of the Incarnation.

"An Augustinian? But what made you change your mind, Rose? I thought you didn't want to go into a convent."

"Ssh, Ferdinand! You mustn't let anyone know about this."

"You mean you haven't told Father or Mother?"

The girl shook her head. "No," she said slowly. "Just now only my confessor at Santo Domingo knows about it—Father Alonso Velasquez."

"And what does he think?"

"He didn't say much—just gave me his blessing and a few words of advice."

The young man looked at his sister thoughtfully. Better than anyone else in the family, he knew how faithfully she had given herself to prayer and good works. It had always been that way, even when they were small children. And now she was about to make the greatest sacrifice of all.

"You're sad about something, Ferdinand."

"Not exactly. But I'm going to miss you, Rose. I can't imagine what it's going to be like to come home and not find you somewhere about. You've always been here when I wanted you. Now if I want to talk to you there'll be bars between us; maybe other nuns listening to what I say. That's the way it is in convents, isn't it?"

"Hush! Someone may hear you."

"What if they do? They'll have to know sometime."

"I wish," cried Rose, "I could tell the whole world right now. But Father Alonso says to keep it a secret. Even from Father and Mother. By the way, will you do me a little favor?"

"What?"

"The Mother Abbess expects me at the convent next Sunday afternoon. Will you take me there, Ferdinand? I can't very well walk over by myself."

The young man nodded. It was the Spanish custom that no girl of good family should ever walk through the streets unescorted. Many a time he had had to accompany Rose on a visit to some church or convent.

"Of course I'll take you," he said quickly. "Maybe such a good deed will go down in history."

For the rest of the week Rose was very busy, and not only with her flowers. For some time now she had been doing fine sewing and embroidery. Several wealthy ladies were her steady customers, and the money that came in from this new venture was a great help to the family.

"It won't be too different when I've gone away," she told herself, "thanks to Don Gonzalo. What would I do without such a good friend? Not only has he given me a dowry, he's promised to look after the family and see that things go along as usual. Dear Lord, I do thank you for Don Gonzalo! Bless him every day of his life!"

At the hour appointed on Sunday afternoon, Ferdinand and Rose set out for the Monastery of the

Incarnation. It was hard for the girl not to say good-bye to her parents, to her sisters and brothers, to Marianna. But it was not to be. Father Alonso Velasquez feared the arguments that might follow if her intentions were made known to her family.

As the familiar wooden gate clicked shut, Rose turned to her favorite brother. "I hope all this is God's Will, Ferdinand."

"What else could it be?"

"I'm not trying to run away from hardships."

"Of course not! In fact, you're taking more upon yourself by going into a monastery."

As they walked through the streets the girl was silent, gazing for the last time at the squat adobe houses, the beggars, the little Indian children play-ing games. Suddenly a black and white dog darted playfully toward her. Ferdinand threw out a protect-ing arm.

"Be careful, Rose! He may bite you. And he's not too clean."

"He wouldn't bite anyone, Ferdinand. He's only a puppy. But isn't it strange—he's black and white."

"Black and white! There you go again—still thinking about the Dominicans!"

Rose laughed. "Not really, Ferdinand. But I do wish, if there's enough time. . ."

"What?"

"I'd like to go to Santo Domingo for a last visit."

The young man nodded. "All right. We can spare a few minutes, I guess."

Once inside the Dominican church, the brother and sister separated. Ferdinand stayed near the

ROSE REALLY COULD NOT RISE FROM HER KNEES.

back, while his sister went up the right-hand aisle to the Rosary Shrine. She knelt before the golden altar dedicated to Our Lady and once more offered herself as a servant to the Blessed Mother and her Son.

"Help me to be good," she prayed. "Dearest Mother, have mercy on the poor, the suffering, the ignorant. Ask Saint Augustine to pray for me, that I may save many souls as a nun in his holy Order."

As the minutes passed, Ferdinand grew uneasy. Rose was forgetting she had promised to stay only a little while in the Dominican church. The Mother Abbess of the Augustinians had told her to be at the monastery for Vespers. Now, if they walked quickly, they would have just enough time.

He slipped out of the back seat and went rapidly up the aisle. "Rose, it's time we were leaving," he whispered.

The girl looked up. There was very little color in her face and her dark eyes were wide with wonder. "Ferdinand, something's happened! I can't move! It's just as though my knees were glued to the floor!"

"*What?*"

"It's true. Ever since I knelt down I've had to stay in the same spot. There's some strange power holding me here!"

The young man stared. What had happened? Was his sister coming down with some strange illness? Or was she playing a joke on him? One glance at her pale face, however, and he knew that she spoke the truth. Something mysterious had really taken place at Our Lady's shrine. Rose really could not rise from her knees.

"I'll help you," he said in a shaky voice. "Here, take my arm. But be quick about it. Some of the people in church are forgetting to say their prayers. There'll be a crowd over here any minute to see what's wrong."

Rose took her brother's arm, but even the combined efforts of the two young people were in vain. Before the golden altar of Our Lady of the Rosary, with its flowers and flickering wax tapers, Rose remained on her knees.

Ferdinand looked about helplessly. What were they going to do? By now the nuns at the monastery would be waiting for their new Sister. Perhaps they would even send a messenger to the Flores house to see why she had not come. If that happened, Rose's plans would be secret no longer.

"Say a prayer or something," the young man suggested quickly. "There must be some way to get you loose."

Rose looked up at the statue of Our Lady. It had suddenly occurred to her that perhaps God did not wish her to be an Augustinian. Perhaps He had worked this wonder to prove to Don Gonzalo and others that her place was in the world, not in a convent. Perhaps—oh, happy thought!—she was meant to be a Dominican Tertiary after all!

"Dearest Mother, I won't be a nun if it isn't God's Will," she said simply. "I'll go back home and live with my family. I'll do my very best to serve Him well there. Only please let me get up!"

The words were no sooner out than Rose knew she could rise to her feet. Her brother stared as she stood up beside him.

"But what happened, Rose? How were you able to get up after all?"

The girl's dark eyes were shining. "*She* did it, Ferdinand—the Blessed Mother! She doesn't want me to go to the monastery this afternoon. She wants me to go home. I heard her voice in my heart."

The young man shook his head. What was the Mother Abbess of the Augustinians going to say to all this? And Don Gonzalo de Massa?

CHAPTER 9

A DAUGHTER OF SAINT DOMINIC

I T WAS a few weeks later, on August 10, the feast of Saint Laurence, that Rose joined the Dominican Order as a Tertiary. Her face was radiant as she knelt before the Rosary Shrine in Santo Domingo and heard her confessor, Father Alonso Velasquez, begin the ceremony of reception:

> O Lord Jesus Christ, Who didst vouch-safe to clothe Thyself with the garment of our mortality, we beseech Thee, of the abundance of Thy great mercy, that Thou wouldst be pleased so to bless this kind of garment, which the holy Fathers have appointed to be worn in token of inno-cence and humility, that she who is to be clothed with it may be worthy to put on Thee, Christ Our Lord.

Rose looked up at the garment Father Alonso was blessing. It was the Dominican habit of white wool, spread out now upon the altar—the very same type of dress once worn by Saint Catherine of Siena and other holy souls. In a few minutes this white habit would be hers to wear, instead of the fine clothes of her mother's choice.

How good God was to bless a poor Peruvian girl with the vocation of a Dominican Tertiary. In just a few minutes she would no longer be alone in the task of saving her own soul and the souls of others. The prayers of Dominicans everywhere—priests, nuns, lay Brothers, other Tertiaries—would be joined to hers in a very special way.

Rose shut her eyes in sheer happiness as Father Alonso sprinkled her with Holy Water and continued the prayer:

> May the Lord also sprinkle thee with hyssop, who art now going to be clothed with our garments, that thou mayest be made clean, so that being thus cleansed and made whiter than snow in thy soul, thou mayest so appear outwardly in our habit. . . .

Maria de Oliva, kneeling a few feet away, dabbed her tearful eyes. This certainly was not what she had planned for her favorite child—a life in the world as a lay member of a religious Order. Yet what could she do? The girl absolutely refused to be interested in marriage. All she cared about was saving souls.

"Perhaps she'll change her mind in a little while," the mother told herself between sobs. "Perhaps after a few months she'll find the Tertiary life too hard."

But Rose of Saint Mary, the new Tertiary daughter of Saint Dominic, was happier than she had ever been before. At last she was walking the same road walked by Saint Catherine of Siena nearly two hundred and fifty years before. Even Don Gonzalo was satisfied, as the months passed, that Rose had chosen the right path. Although other men and women might be called to the religious life, her vocation was to become a saint in the world. Never again would he urge that she be a nun in any of Lima's five convents.

"God has given that girl a very special work," Don Gonzalo told himself. "She is to be a model for all who must reach perfection without the help of the cloister."

On August 10, 1607, Rose returned to the Rosary Shrine at Santo Domingo. Her one year's probation as a Tertiary was over. Was she willing to continue the life? asked Father Alonso Velasquez. Was she willing to make a promise to live according to the Rule of the Dominican Order until she died?

The girl, now twenty-one years old, had not a single doubt concerning her Tertiary profession. As Rose of Saint Mary, she gave the necessary promise. Now she was a real member of the Dominican Order.

Time passed. To all outward appearances Rose seemed changed very little: she still lived quietly at home, raising her flowers and doing fine sewing for the wealthy women of Lima. Yet a change was

IN A FEW MINUTES THIS WHITE HABIT
WOULD BE HERS TO WEAR.

taking place, nevertheless. Little by little, through devoutly receiving the Holy Eucharist, through patiently bearing trials and troubles, Gaspar's daughter was slowly becoming more like Christ. Sometimes when her mother argued that she took too little care of her health, she answered gently:

"You and I shall live as long as God wishes, Mother. When our work for Him is done, then we can worry about our health."

"Who's going to think about such things then?" demanded Maria sharply. "It'll be too late."

Rose smoothed the folds of her white woolen habit. "Mother dear, life is really very simple if only we remember that we are servants—servants of God and our neighbor."

"*Servants?* Who wants to be a servant? Rose, such talk is disgusting! At that rate, a Negro or an Indian is as good as a white man! And a person with money and education is no better than an ignorant beggar! To think that you talk this way— after all I've done for you..."

Rose took a deep breath. "Mother, please don't be angry! I'm only trying to help a little. After all, if we really believe that God is our Father and His Son our Brother..."

"Enough of your preaching, young lady. Ever since you became a Tertiary you've been far too pious to suit me. Just remember this: I don't want to hear any more talk about being a servant. Your father may be poor but he comes from a good family. And so do I!"

The failure of this and other conversations proved

to Rose what she had always known—that relief for
the lonely heart can be found in prayer. In prayer,
weak human nature reaches out for God and
becomes strong with His help. Troubles of all kinds,
when they are offered to Him in union with the
sufferings His Son knew on earth, turn into merit
of untold value. That was one reason why there was
so much sorrow in the world: without pain very few
souls would ever think of turning to God.

"Everyone wants to be happy," Rose often
thought. "That's why we were made. But how hard
it is to remember that we can only be satisfied with
the greatest good of all—God Himself!"

On Palm Sunday of the year 1610, when she was
twenty-four years old, Rose went to Mass at Santo
Domingo. The ceremony was a long one, with the
blessing of the Palms and the procession through
the church preceding the Holy Sacrifice. As two lay
Brothers finished distributing the blessed Palm to
the people, the choir broke into a triumphant hymn
and everyone made ready to join in the procession.

Rose hesitated. Somehow or other she had been
overlooked in the distribution of the green
branches. She alone, of all the people in Santo
Domingo, had no piece of blessed Palm.

"Why?" she thought. "Can it be that I'm not
worthy to walk with the others?"

She thrust her disappointment aside, however. It
was only a mistake—the lay Brothers had been too
busy to notice her. There was no reason why she
could not walk in the procession, too. Even though
she had no Palm branch to carry, she could still call

to mind the first Palm Sunday, when Our Lord had entered Jerusalem amid the welcome of His happy followers.

When the choir finally finished singing and the long line of people returned to their seats, Rose cast a swift glance at the Rosary Shrine. How she loved this statue of Our Lady holding her Infant Son! Here, four years ago, she had received the Blessed Mother's approval of her vocation to the Third Order of Saint Dominic. That Sunday afternoon when she had been forced to remain on her knees before the golden altar, a voice had spoken in her heart. It had told her she was not called to work out her salvation in a monastery. Rather, she was to stay in the world—she was to be a saint amid everyday surroundings. She would spend her time praying, helping with the housework, sewing, working in the garden, and caring for the sick poor.

"Dearest Mother, thank you again for letting me be a Dominican Tertiary," she whispered. "And I'm not sad about the lay Brothers' forgetting to give me a Palm branch. The Palm I really want is the one that will never fade, the one you give to the blessed in Heaven."

As Rose breathed this little prayer, her startled eyes suddenly beheld the Blessed Mother smile and turn lovingly toward the Child in her arms. No one else in the crowded church saw the wonder, nor did they hear the words which the Child presently uttered—words which echoed in the girl's heart like the sweetest music:

"Rose of My Heart, be thou My spouse!"

Rose saw and heard, however, and her heart filled with pure joy. God had blessed her with still another wonderful gift! In her beloved Dominican church He had told her that she was really numbered among His chosen ones!

"It's too much!" she whispered. "I'm not worthy of such love."

Yet she knew she had not been mistaken about the vision. She, a poor girl of Peru, had been chosen from all eternity to belong to God, to be one of His especially beloved friends forever and ever. She had read of such favors being given to others, including her dear patroness, Saint Catherine of Siena. Now, through a miracle of grace, the marvelous honor was to be hers, too.

For the rest of the day Rose could think of little else. When Ferdinand remarked that she seemed very happy, she nodded.

"It's quite true—I am. And I've another favor to ask."

The young man laughed. "I suppose you want me to take you some place?"

"No, I just want you to make me a ring."

"A ring? *You* want a piece of jewelry?"

"That's right. But nothing from the markets. Just a plain ring of your own design. Ferdinand, you will do this for me? It's really so very important."

As the young man looked at his sister's eager face, he realized that something unusual had taken place. For years Rose had been thinking constantly of other people—praying for them, helping out when they were sick, seeing that the poor had all the flowers and fruit she could spare from the garden. Now the time had finally come when she wanted something for herself.

"Of course I'll get you a ring. Do you want it of silver or of gold? And what's your favorite stone?"

Rose hesitated. Both metals were common in Peru. And diamonds and emeralds were common, too, being found in abundance in the mines of the Andes. She could have a really beautiful ring without very much expense.

"I'd like a gold ring, Ferdinand. But without any stone. Just a plain gold band."

"How about having a little motto on it? A few words engraved on the outside? That could be easily done."

"What words would you suggest?"

The young man thought a moment. "How about this: 'Rose of My Heart, be thou My spouse'?"

The girl's heart filled. She could not express her great emotion. Without realizing it, her brother had been divinely inspired to choose the very words she had heard in church—the words spoken to her that morning by the Child Jesus Himself.

"Well, what's the matter? Don't you like my idea?"

"Ferdinand, it's beautiful! I can't think of anything I'd like better."

"All right. We'll have a plain gold ring made for you, with those words on the outside. I know the very jeweler to do the job, too—an old friend of mine who hasn't been very busy lately."

Rose smiled gratefully. "And he can make the ring soon?"

"Of course. Probably in a couple of days. I'll go to see him tomorrow with a sketch of what we want."

When she was once more alone, Rose sought out her little oratory at the back of the garden. It was always quiet and peaceful here. Only infrequently did anyone else in the family come down among the banana trees. There were too many spiders and mosquitoes, they said. Besides, the sun very rarely penetrated the dense tangle of vines and branches. It was a dark and gloomy place at best.

Rose was not afraid of the spiders and mosquitoes, however. She had never once harmed them, and they seemed eager to show her their friendship. Whenever she said the Rosary or her other prayers in her little oratory, the mosquitoes buzzed in a most friendly fashion. It was almost as though they were trying to pray, too. As for the spiders, they stopped their wanderings and their weavings: they would do these things when their young friend had finished talking to God.

Rose was not thinking of spiders or mosquitoes, however, as she entered her little shrine. Rather it was of the wonderful grace that had been given to her that morning in the Dominican church. And of course there was the ring—the beautiful golden ring she would always wear to remind herself that she belonged to God. How could she forget that?

"This is Palm Sunday," she thought. "If my ring is ready by Wednesday, perhaps Father Alonso could put it in the Repository on Holy Thursday. How wonderful that would be!"

Yes, it would be wonderful. But unusual, too. Probably it would take quite a lot of explaining to make her confessor understand.

"I'll do my best," she resolved within herself. "Our Lord is hidden in the Repository on Holy Thursday. I want my ring to be with Him then. On Easter Sunday, when He comes back to us in glory, I will take my ring and wear it until I die!"

CHAPTER 10

THE HERMIT

ON THE morning of July 14, a few months after Rose received her golden ring, the bells of Lima sent their mournful music over the city once again. The holy Franciscan missionary, Father Francis Solano, was dead.

Listening to the somber sound, Maria de Oliva muttered a brief prayer. "We'd better go at once to the Franciscan convent, Marianna. I'm sure there'll be miracles over there today. Get all our rosaries and medals. We can touch them to the body of Father Francis and use them as relics."

The Indian woman nodded. Both mistress and servant realized the loss. Father Francis Solano was a real saint. Back in 1589, when he had first come to the New World, he and his companions had been shipwrecked off the coast of Colombia. For weeks the little group of survivors wandered through the coastal forests without meeting a soul. Then a few of the men died from eating poisonous plants, and despair seized the rest. Only Father Francis remained calm. He insisted that his companions stay near the coast. Another boat would arrive from Panama soon, he assured them, and carry them safely to Peru.

"I remember when he finally did reach Lima," said Marianna slowly. "We were so disappointed when he insisted on leaving almost at once. Ah, *señora,* he was already weak from hardship, yet he thought nothing of walking fourteen hundred miles, across mountains and jungles, to his Franciscan mission in Argentina!"

"And he made that trip twice, Marianna. Don't forget that."

"*Sí, señora*—eleven years later, when his hard work among the Indians was finished. Ah, but he was a good soul! I'll go now and find the rosaries and medals."

Out in the garden, among her beloved trees and flowers, Rose was thinking of Father Francis, too. She would never forget that December day in the year 1604 when the brown-clad friar had preached his famous sermon in the market place. She had been just eighteen then. Now, six years later, the memory was still fresh.

"He told people to do penance for their sins," she recalled. "He insisted that God would destroy Lima unless they ceased to offend Him. That night there weren't enough priests in the city to hear everyone who wanted to go to confession. Enemies were reconciled, stolen goods restored to their owners, three thousand marriages properly ratified. Ah, dear Father Francis, give me some of that zeal for souls which you so truly possessed!"

Having offered her brief prayer, Rose turned down the path that led to the back of the garden. There a familiar figure awaited her.

"Doña Maria! Why, I didn't expect to see you this morning!"

Doña Maria de Usátegui, the wife of Don Gonzalo, gave Rose an affectionate embrace. "My dear, I came in quietly by the side gate. Your mother doesn't know I'm here yet. You see, I wanted to have a word with you alone."

"The children aren't sick again?"

"No, no. They're fine. Rose, my dear, how would you like to live with Don Gonzalo and me? Be a daughter of ours, so to speak?"

The young woman stared at her visitor in amazement. "I don't understand..."

"Of course you don't. But my husband and I both feel you'd be happier with us. Since your mother can't understand the type of life you want, since she's never been happy that you joined the Third Order of Saint Dominic..."

Rose laughed. No one would have guessed that Doña Maria's words cut through her like a knife. They were so true! Maria de Oliva never lost an opportunity to show she did not approve of Dominican Tertiaries.

"Mother just doesn't understand yet. She finds it hard to believe that I'm still myself, underneath this white habit."

"Exactly. I've heard some of her criticisms and so has my husband. Dear little friend, we've a large house and plenty of this world's goods. Why don't you come and live with us? The children would be so happy!"

For the rest of the day, and for many days thereafter, Rose pondered this kindly offer of Doña Maria de Usátegui. In the end she decided to decline. Even though Maria de Oliva frequently found fault with Dominican Tertiary life, with the prayers and sacrifices to which her daughter was dedicated, Rose knew such trials could be turned into great merit.

"Long ago I offered to pray and suffer for others," she thought. "Dear Lord, don't let me run away from any pain now. Let Mother's failure to understand only bring me closer to You. Let it help to make me a saint."

The weeks passed, with their ceaseless round of ordinary activities. Always clad in her white Tertiary habit and veil, Rose tended her flowers and herbs, did her fine sewing and embroidery. She was completely unaware of the rumors spreading throughout the city to the effect that she was quite as holy as those other great servants of God, Archbishop Turribius, Father Francis Solano, and Brother Martin de Porres. Hardly a day passed that men and women did not come to beg her prayers, to ask her advice on one subject or another, to touch her famous statue of the Child Jesus, which she called "The Little Doctor."

"Rose is another Saint Catherine of Siena," they told one another. "She fasts all the time. She sleeps only two hours a night. She has given her whole self to the saving of sinners."

Eventually, however, some of all this did reach the young woman's ears. Quickly she went in search of her mother with a strange request. She wanted permission to be a hermit in the garden. If she cut herself off from the world, if she appeared only rarely in the streets, perhaps people would forget about her. But since the little oratory she had made as a child, far back among the banana trees, was nearly in ruins, it would be necessary to build another. And this second hermitage would have to be of more durable material—with a door that would lock.

Maria de Oliva refused to listen to any such suggestion. It was bad enough to see her pretty daughter in a religious habit, to know that she had thrown away forever the chance to have a husband and children. But that she should live as a hermit in a little adobe house in the garden—never!

Four years passed. Rose did not give up hope of having her little adobe house. Finally, overcome by the pleadings of Father Alonso Velasquez, Doña Maria de Usátegui and Don Gonzalo, her mother gave in. Yes—Rose could bury herself as a hermit, if Father Alonso thought this the proper thing to do. She could stop having visitors. She could ruin her health by spending hours in a damp mud hut.

"Mother, how can I ever thank you?" cried the girl. "I've wanted it for so long!"

Maria sighed as she looked at her daughter, now twenty-eight years of age. She was still pretty, but far too thin. The white Dominican habit could not hide the fact that for years Rose had been following a very difficult life.

"Sometimes I can't understand why you didn't enter a convent, child. What other girl in Lima prays as much as you?"

Rose laughed, remembering that Sunday afternoon at Santo Domingo when a mysterious power had kept her kneeling at the Rosary Shrine. "It was never my vocation to be a nun, Mother. Please believe me. And please pray that I serve God well as a hermit."

"I'll pray," said the mother sadly. "But just remember this—if it hadn't been that Father Alonso thought it the thing to do, I'd never have given my permission. It's—it's such an odd kind of life for a young woman!"

For the next few days Rose and Ferdinand were very busy. A site had been chosen for the hermitage, closer to the house this time, and not cut off from the sunlight. An area five feet by four had been traced on the ground, and near at hand was a supply of rough adobe bricks. They were light brown in color and not too heavy to lift.

"Ferdinand, what would I do without you?" said Rose as the two set to work on the proposed cell. "You've always been so good to me, ever since we were small."

"It's no great trouble to build this little place, Rose. The only thing that worries me is how you're going to be able to live in such a tiny house. Couldn't we make it just a little bigger?"

The girl shook her head. "I want it small so there won't be room for many visitors. And just one tiny window."

"What about the door? How do you want that?"

"I have special plans for the door. It's to be very low, and just big enough for a person to crawl through on his hands and knees. You see, the smaller and more uncomfortable we make this little cell, the fewer people will want to come and see me."

The young man smiled. This was certainly true. Not many of his mother's friends, for example, would want to crawl through a tiny door on their knees.

"You tell me what you wish and that's the way it will be, Rose. I want you to have happy memories of me when you come to live in this little hermitage."

"Memories? You're not going away, Ferdinand?"

"Yes. I'm going to Chile next month."

"On business?"

"No, I plan to join the army. After all, I'm thirty years old and it's time I settled down somewhere."

Rose checked her surprise and disappointment. This favorite brother spoke the truth. Most men his age were already married, with homes and families of their own. Yet she would miss him so much. . . .

"I'll pray for you every day," she said gently. "No matter where you go, my prayers will follow you. And I'm sure you'll like living in Chile, Ferdinand. You'll marry a nice girl. . .and you'll have a beautiful little daughter. . . ."

"What are you talking about?" the man asked incredulously.

"You're going to name the little girl after me.

THE ADOBE HERMITAGE WAS AT LAST FINISHED.

She'll be called Mary Rose."

"Well," said Ferdinand, laughing heartily, "you're right about one thing: if I ever do have a daughter, she'll have your name. Who knows—maybe some day she'll even visit this little hermitage!"

Rose smiled at him. Although he did not guess it, her brother spoke the truth. Mary Rose would indeed come to Lima one day, a very famous little girl.

After a few more days of hard work, the adobe hermitage was at last finished. The younger Flores children had great fun crawling in and out of the tiny door, and standing on a chair to look through the one small window that opened onto the garden. Friends and neighbors, and even several priests, came to view the adobe house which Rose and Ferdinand had made. A few even measured the dimensions to make sure their eyes were not playing tricks.

"Five feet long, four feet wide, six feet high!" declared Father Alonso Velasquez in amazement. "Rose, it's far too small!"

"Father, it's large enough for Our Lord and me. I think I'll be very happy here."

Doña Maria de Usátegui, who was also among the visitors inspecting the hermitage, laid an affectionate hand on the younger woman's shoulder. "The invitation still stands," she whispered. "My husband and I still want you to come and live with us. You'll let us know if you change your mind?"

Rose nodded. Don Gonzalo and Doña Maria were such very good friends. She knew they both

worried about her health, about the life of hardship
to which she had dedicated herself.

"I won't forget the invitation," she smiled. "Or
your other kindnesses, either. Thank you so much
for everything, Doña Maria."

After she had begun to live in the little hermitage, Rose continued to work at her sewing, her
embroidery, the raising of flowers and herbs. When
night came, however, she shut herself in and gave
herself over to prayer. There, amid the silence of
the darkened garden, she poured out her heart in
praise and petition.

Such actions were pleasing to God, and He
flooded the new hermit's soul with many graces.
Frequently He appeared to her as a little Child,
encouraging her to continue with her difficult vocation. He taught her she had nothing to fear as long
as she put all her confidence in Him.

At such times Rose thought she would die of
sheer happiness. What a wonderful thing life is, she
told herself. Any soul that has Sanctifying Grace,
no matter how weak the soul is, can be of use to
its fellows. All that is necessary is to think of God
and His goodness. Then will come such an urge to
be like Him, to share in His truth and beauty, that
the soul cannot help exchanging its cowardice for
courage. It begins to resemble God. And because
of that, it glows with a great love for other souls.
It wants them to have Sanctifying Grace and to love
God, too. It wants them to share its happiness.

"It's like a beggar who finally becomes rich,"
Rose would reflect. "When he is poor, he is afraid

of other people. He has a low opinion of himself, knowing he can never do anything great. But once he becomes a rich man, everything is changed. His starved body becomes strong. He realizes other people look up to him. And he finds real happiness in sharing his wealth with them."

One summer afternoon Maria de Oliva went in search of her daughter. The sun was warm and the garden bright with the flowers Rose tended so well. But the woman's face as she made her way toward the little adobe hermitage was hard with anger.

"Rose! Are you in there?"

There was no answer. Catching a glimpse of someone moving among the fruit trees, Maria started off in that direction. Probably Rose was gathering oranges for Marianna to take to market the next day.

"Rose! Are you deaf? Haven't you heard me calling you?"

The girl set down a basket half full of luscious fruit. "Did you want me, Mother?"

"I certainly did. Doña Isabel de Mejía came to see me. She has told me something that's upset me dreadfully."

"Her mother's not sick again?"

"Of course not. I'm the one that's sick. Rose, is it true you've told people there's going to be a convent of Dominican nuns in Lima? That Doña Lucia de la Daga will be the first Prioress?"

A smile lit up the young woman's face. "Yes, Mother. It will be called the Monastery of Santa Catalina, after Saint Catherine of Siena."

Maria's voice was shrill. "Doña Lucia is a happily married woman, with five lovely children! What business have you to spread the rumor that she's going to be a nun?"

"But it's true, Mother. There *will* be a Monastery of Santa Catalina. Doña Lucia will go there with her sister Clara. Father Luis de Bilbao will say the first Mass. . . ."

"So you're turning into a prophet, are you? What do you know about the future? Are you losing your senses since you've shut yourself up in that wretched hermitage?"

Rose lowered her eyes. How could she make her mother understand that the news about Santa Catalina had been given to her in prayer? That her beloved friend and patroness, Saint Catherine of Siena, had come in person to tell her about the new monastery?

"I'm sorry, Mother. I didn't realize you'd be so upset about what I told Doña Isabel."

"Why shouldn't I be upset? What's Doña Lucia going to think of me? And her husband? Why, you've really said the good man is going to die. . .and his five children, too. Otherwise how could Doña Lucia enter a convent?"

Rose smiled faintly. "Please don't be cross, Mother. Things really will happen as I've said."

"Stop!" cried Maria. "Soon you'll be telling people that your own mother is going to found a convent. I won't have such talk, Rose. It's too embarrassing!"

The girl looked down at the golden ring which

Ferdinand had obtained for her four years ago. There were tears in her eyes.

"You won't found a monastery, Mother, but some day you'll enter one. Doña Lucia will give you the Dominican habit at Santa Catalina. You'll be very happy there. And I promise you that when you're ready to die, I'll come to get you myself."

CHAPTER 11

A NEW HOME

MARIA WAS almost beside herself at Rose's words. She a Dominican nun? Never! Yet the young Tertiary refused to listen to the protests of her mother. One day, when the Monastery of Santa Catalina was a reality, Maria de Oliva would go there to ask for the Dominican habit. She would spend her last years in God's service.

The months passed and Rose continued her hermit's life. There were times, however, when she confided to some of her friends that her real desire was to be a martyr.

"If I were a man, I'd like nothing better than to be a missionary," she told Frances de Montoya, a young woman about her own age. "Just think how many missionaries have gone straight to Heaven because they died at the hands of savages!"

Frances shivered. Although she, too, belonged to the Third Order of Saint Dominic, she had always found it hard to practice mortifications—even very small ones. Indeed, her visits to Rose caused her much concern. There were so many mosquitoes in the garden of Gaspar Flores. They filled the adobe hermitage and Frances always emerged with a great number of painful bites.

"I'd never be brave enough to want a martyr's death," she sighed. "I can't even stand being bitten by these mosquitoes of yours."

Rose smiled. "Yet you still come to see me, Frances. How do you explain that, if you're so afraid of suffering?"

"But this is different! You don't know how much better I feel after a talk with you! I'm so grateful you still let me come, Rose, even though you really don't want a lot of visitors. There's just one thing I wonder about."

"What?"

"Why don't the mosquitoes bite your mother? Or Doña Maria de Usátegui? Or you?"

"Because we've promised never to hurt these little guests."

"*Guests?* Is that what you call these wretched insects?"

Rose nodded. "Suppose you make the promise, too, Frances. Then you won't be bitten any more."

The visitor looked ruefully at her arm. Already there were three red marks on it. "If I could have a little peace when I come to see you, I'd promise anything."

"All right. Offer the pain of these three bites for the Poor Souls, in honor of the Blessed Trinity. Then make your promise."

Frances could not help laughing. "I'll never kill

any of your guests again," she announced firmly. "I just hope they understand what I'm saying."

Rose smiled. Of course the little creatures understood. From now on Frances de Montoya would be one more person who could visit the adobe hermitage in peace.

On April 30, 1615, Rose had her twenty-ninth birthday. Some weeks later she was surprised to find her small garden retreat surrounded by an excited mob. Women were crying. Men—husbands and sons—were pale with fear. Word had just been received that a fleet of Dutch pirate ships was anchored off the harbor of Callao. This seaport, only ten miles from Lima, was poorly defended. Probably the newcomers would begin a successful invasion at any moment.

"Rose, you must pray hard!" cried Don Gonzalo de Massa. "The Dutch intend to seize our gold and silver, our slaves, even our children!"

"They're Calvinists," put in his wife, Doña Maria. "They believe it's their duty to kill every Catholic they can find."

Doctor John del Castillo, one of the finest physicians in Lima, nodded. "They'll burn the churches first," he declared. "They have a great hatred for the Blessed Sacrament, Rose. They've committed dreadful outrages in other cities. My dear, will you pray as you've never prayed before?"

Rose had come out of her hermitage. There were a great many people in the garden, and fear was stamped on every face.

"Of course I'll pray," she said quietly. "But

there's no real reason to be alarmed. The Dutch won't try to land at Callao. They won't fire on the town, either."

In vain Don Gonzalo described the dreadful things done by pirates in Panama and other Spanish colonies. Rose insisted that during the night the enemy fleet would lift anchor and sail away from Callao. But the crowd found her words hard to believe, and in the end she agreed to pray for Lima's safety, to ask the special protection of Saint Mary Magdalen, whose feast would occur the next day.

All night the city made ready for the expected attack. Couriers kept arriving from Callao with the latest news. Special services were ordered in all the churches. Confessionals were crowded. The scene was much like that which had taken place eleven years before, when a sermon by Father Francis Solano had converted enormous numbers of sinners. Fear and anxiety filled the hearts of everyone—Spaniard, Indian and Negro. No one cared to go to bed that night. People flocked to the churches instead, or followed the numerous processions of the Blessed Sacrament which wound through the darkened streets.

Having received permission from Father Alonso Velasquez to leave her little hermitage, Rose hurried to Santo Domingo with a few women friends. Her heart was torn between two desires. If the Dutch pirates were allowed to attack Lima, she might have the chance to die as a martyr. Since they were not, thousands of lives would be saved.

Yet, as she found a place in the crowded Chapel of Saint Jerome in the Dominican church, she smiled at the thought of obtaining a martyr's crown and going straight to Heaven. Certainly if the Dutch were to come, she would make no effort to hide from them. With her rosary in her hand, she would give her life in defense of the Blessed Sacrament.

When the grey dawn finally lifted, it was upon a very different scene from that of the night before. People were singing in the streets. Gone were the anxiety and fear of a few hours before. The latest message from Callao had stated that some time during the night the Dutch ships had lifted anchor, and were now no longer to be seen.

"It's a miracle!" Doña Maria de Usátegui told her husband. "And I'm sure our little Rose is responsible! Gonzalo, don't you think she may have offered her life to spare Lima from destruction?"

Don Gonzalo nodded. "I wouldn't be surprised," he said. "She has more courage and charity than any other girl I know."

There were others who shared the same opinion. Presently, to the accompaniment of joyful church bells, the air was echoing with one cry:

"The prayers of Rose Flores have saved us from harm!"

In the company of her mother and friends, Rose went slowly homeward. She was tired and a little confused. Why did people think her prayers so powerful? Didn't they realize they owed their deliverance to God's mercy? She, Rose Flores, was

SHE SMILED AT THE THOUGHT OF
GOING STRAIGHT TO HEAVEN.

less than dust and not worthy of any honor.

"But I'm glad you saved the city, Lord," she thought. "And I'm not too sad that You didn't let me be a martyr. After all, You do give a kind of martyrdom to everyone in this world. It's a rather plain sort, without swords or bullets or fire—just our many little trials and troubles. If we bear these cheerfully, we can please You as much as the holy martyrs do."

It was a few days later that Father Alonso Velasquez came to his young friend's hermitage. He had some very special news. Rose was to leave her parents' house and go to live with Don Gonzalo and his wife. Doña Maria had been to see him recently, asserting that Rose's health was failing; that the hermit's life was too hard for her.

"You're lucky that Don Gonzalo and Doña Maria think so much of you," said Father Alonso. "They're very wealthy people and their one wish is to see you strong and well. You'll have a very fine home with them."

Rose could not hide her distress. "But how can I leave my own family, Father? My parents aren't young anymore. They need me."

The priest smiled. "You understand what obedience is, Rose. It is my wish that you put an end to the hardships in your life. I want you to go to the de Massas' and try to build up your health."

Rose was silent. As a member of the Dominican family, she owed obedience to her Superiors. If Father Alonso thought it best for her to live elsewhere, she had no choice but to do as he wished.

"I'll go," she answered. "But I'm not really sick, Father. Our Lord has given me more than two years in which to serve Him."

"You'll live longer than that, my child, if only you take care of yourself. From now on you're to think more about your health."

So Rose went to live with Don Gonzalo and Doña Maria. From the start she assured these two good friends that she wanted only a plain little room and that she wished to be of use as a nurse to their younger children.

Micaela and Beatrice, the two older daughters, tried to make the newcomer feel she was their honored guest, that there was no need for her to work in her new home. Their efforts met with little success, however. Rose had been in love with humility too long.

"She's a real saint," Micaela told her mother. "I wouldn't be surprised if she's canonized as soon as she dies."

"We're really lucky to have her here," put in Beatrice. "Some day this house of ours will be famous. People will come from all over the world just to see the little room where Rose lived."

Doña Maria nodded. "There's not a day passes that I don't thank God for letting her come into our family. She does worry me a little, though. . . ."

"You mean because she says she's going to die in two years? On Saint Bartholomew's day?"

"That's right. She'll be only thirty-one years old then. That's far too early for her to leave us."

Don Gonzalo reassured his wife. "With good

food and plenty of rest, it'll be a different story, Maria. Just look at her father. He's ninety-three. If Rose takes after him, she'll be with us for a long, long time."

So the days passed. Rose missed her little garden cell, and the flowers and trees she had loved to tend, but she still kept busy. For years she had been an expert at needlework. In the de Massa house she continued this activity, making clothes for the younger children and altar linens for various churches. From time to time she also entertained the family and servants by playing the harp, the zither and the guitar. Her voice was sweet and clear, and everyone enjoyed her songs.

Father Alonso had insisted that she was not to tire herself with too many prayers or sacrifices, so all in all Rose now led a somewhat easier life. Yet she never forgot how she had dedicated herself to saving souls from Hell. Not an hour passed that she did not offer some short prayer for sinners. One of her favorites was the beginning of Psalm 69: "Incline unto my aid, O God; O Lord, make haste to help me." There were numerous short ejaculations, too. They took little time to say and were richly indulgenced.

Most of all, however, there was the Holy Sacrifice of the Mass—the greatest prayer of all. When she had been a hermit in her father's garden, Rose had been given a very wonderful grace: She had been privileged to hear in spirit, through the window of her little cell, all the Masses being offered in Lima's churches. Now that she was a member of Don

Gonzalo's family, the wonderful grace continued, and the young Dominican Tertiary always applied the merit of these Masses to the welfare of others.

Sometimes Doña Maria regarded her guest a little fearfully. It was a great honor to have Rose living in the house, yet a little frightening, too. The girl worked miracles so openly; she conversed with saints and angels, and people were always coming to the door to ask for prayers and to report cures of various kinds. These clients of hers were not only the poor and ignorant. They included, for instance, no less a person than the Prior of the Dominican Convent of Saint Mary Magdalen, Father Bartholomew Martínez. This holy priest insisted he had been cured of a grievous illness because Rose had offered some prayers for him at Santo Domingo.

There was also the case of Maria Euphemia de Pareja and her only son, Roderick. Although the mother had always wanted her boy to be a Jesuit priest, Roderick showed little inclination for the religious life. As time passed, Maria Euphemia sadly admitted the truth: her boy was interested only in worldly pleasures. Finally she came to Rose. Surely if the holy woman prayed, Roderick would receive the grace of a religious vocation.

"And that's just what happened," Doña Maria thought to herself. "Overnight the boy reformed. He decided to be a priest, although in the Franciscan Order, not the Society of Jesus. Today his mother's so proud of him! I don't think she'll ever stop being grateful for the prayers Rose said."

As the months passed, Doña Maria often found herself watching Rose closely. The girl seemed well, yet there was something about her that caused the older woman to worry. It was now the year 1617. Could it be true that God would soon call her to Heaven?

"I just can't bear to lose her!" thought the good woman. "She's become another daughter to me."

Rose felt sorry at her adopted mother's grief. One April morning she approached her rather humbly. "Doña Maria, when I come to die I'll be tormented by great thirst. Will you give me water when I ask for it?"

A shiver ran through the older woman. "Of course, my child. But don't talk about dying. You're enjoying much better health here lately."

Rose smiled. "There's another thing, too. I want you and my mother to be the only ones to prepare my body for burial."

Doña Maria stared, then burst into tears. The feast of Saint Bartholomew was now so close! Only four months...

"Don't say such things!" she begged. "Life will never be the same if you leave me, Rose!"

The good woman's fears began to fade, however, as summer approached. Rose had become the picture of health. Even Father Alonso Velasquez agreed that she was looking very well.

"I should have sent her to you long ago," he told Doña Maria. "The life she led at home was far too hard."

The woman nodded vigorously. "You're right,

Father. The Flores' servant, Marianna, was here the
other day. What stories she told me of Rose's
prayers and sacrifices! I still don't understand how
anyone could do so much."

The priest smiled. "It's been going on for years,
Doña Maria—ever since Rose was eleven and saw
with her own eyes the paganism existing among the
Indians who live in the Andes. At that time she
heard Archbishop Turribius prophesy that Quivi
would be destroyed. I know what those words
meant to her. And then came the earthquake and
the floods of 1601; she's never forgotten the
hundreds of people who perished miserably at
Quivi as a punishment for mocking the Archbishop
and the Faith he tried to bring them. Since then
her whole life has been dedicated to saving souls
through prayer and suffering."

Counseled by the Dominican priest not to worry
about Rose's prophecy of approaching death, Doña
Maria and her household breathed more easily. And
when, late in July, Rose asked permission to visit
her garden hermitage, they thought nothing of it.
During the night of August 1, however, the whole
house was awakened by pitiful cries coming from
her room. Rushing to investigate, Doña Maria found
her guest sticken with a mortal illness. She could
scarcely breathe, and her whole body was
paralyzed.

At once the woman sent for Doctor John del
Castillo, and for the various priests whom Rose
knew well. Doña Maria's husband tried to comfort
his wife, but she clutched his arm frantically.

"She's going to die, Gonzalo! And there's not a thing we can do for her!"

The treasurer of the city of Lima, whose wealth and high social position made him a noted figure throughout Peru, could scarcely control his own grief. For the past two years, ever since she had come to live in his house, Rose had seemed so well and happy. Now there was this calamity, this spectacle of a young and beautiful woman called home long before her time.

"She's resting more easily now that Father John de Lorenzana has anointed her," he thought. "Perhaps, if she's nursed carefully. . ."

But Rose only smiled as she saw the many medicines brought to save her life. One damp August day succeeded another, and she repeated again that the feast of Saint Bartholomew would be her last day on earth. The dreadful sufferings now afflicting her body could not be eased. They were part of the payment still required to save certain souls from Hell.

It was on the eve of the Apostle's feast that she stretched out a feeble hand. "Could I see my parents, Doña Maria? I want to say goodbye. And I want to ask forgiveness of everyone in your house for any trouble I may have caused."

The woman nodded hastily. Maria de Oliva was already in the house. And servants had been sent, with a comfortable chair, to carry ninety-five-year-old Gaspar Flores to his daughter's side.

Throughout the day visitors of all sorts passed in and out of Rose's little room—men and women she had befriended, additional doctors summoned in the hope they might give aid, priests of the various religious Orders. Everyone wanted to gaze for the last time on the girl whose sanctity had made her famous throughout the city. Only Doña Maria de Usátegui, tears streaming down her face, refused to leave her side. Rose was asking for water now—and the doctors said she could not have it.

"But I promised! I promised!" Doña Maria kept saying, remembering that April day when Rose had prophesied she would suffer from thirst. "How can I break my word now?"

"Ssh!" murmured Don Gonzalo. "Water would only make her worse."

As midnight approached, Rose turned a gentle glance upon the people kneeling in her room. The deathly pallor was gone from her face now and she seemed more beautiful than ever.

"Please don't feel sad because I'm going to leave you," she whispered. "This is really a happy day."

Maria de Oliva stifled a sob. "Rose, my little one, why didn't I try to understand you better? Forgive me, child, for being so stupid. . . ."

From a corner of the room came the murmur of voices as Don Gonzalo, his wife, and their children repeated the familiar prayers for the dying. Near the door huddled a little group of Negro slaves, their dark faces wet with tears. Rose smiled once again at her friends, then lowered her eyes to the crucifix Father Alonso had given her.

"Jesus, be with me. . ." she murmured.

Quickly Maria de Oliva arose from her knees and

seized a flickering candle. For a moment she stood staring down at the frail figure before her. When she spoke, her voice was surprisingly calm:

"It's—it's all over!" she said.

The others in the room hurried forward. As though a signal had been given, distant bells echoed through the darkness. Midnight! The feast of Saint Bartholomew! And in every one of Lima's monasteries, priests and nuns were starting the new day by chanting the special prayers of the Church in honor of an Apostle.

Maria turned to her companions. There was a strange look of contentment on her tired face.

"My little girl has gone to Heaven," she said quietly.

CHAPTER 12

THE PRIDE OF PERU

DAWN FOUND the streets of Lima filled with people hurrying to Don Gonzalo's house. Word of Rose's death had spread like wildfire, and there was an eager rush to obtain relics. Among the first to arrive was Alfonsa Serrano, a close friend of the dead girl.

"Last night Rose appeared to me!" she declared excitedly. "I was sound asleep. Suddenly, a little after midnight, a bright light shone in my room. In the middle of the light I saw Rose, dressed as a Dominican Tertiary, and shining like the sun. She told me she had just entered Paradise."

Father Alonso Velasquez, together with every other visitor in the de Massa house, listened with interest to what Alfonsa had to say. This girl had been one of Rose's most intimate associates. Indeed, the two had made a bargain some years before: the one who died first was to appear to the other, encouraging her to continue with prayers and good works.

"Rose seems to have kept her word," smiled the

"ROSE IS IN HEAVEN."

priest. "She was dead only a few minutes when she came to tell you about the beauties of Heaven. As far as that goes, she's appeared to several other people, too—among them Doctor John del Castillo."

All morning the crowds streamed in and out of the tiny room where Rose had died. Strangely enough, no one felt sad. The sight of Rose's body, the face more beautiful than they had ever seen it, filled them with joy. There was a strange fragrance, too—as of freshly-cut roses and lilies. It was everywhere in the de Massa house, but especially about the body.

"I don't understand it," Maria de Oliva told Father Alonso. "Surely it isn't coming from that plain little wreath of flowers we put on her head!"

"It's a miracle, *señora*," the priest replied, smiling. "God is taking this way to show us Rose is a saint."

As the hours passed and still more people thronged the house, Doña Maria de Usátegui was repeatedly asked to show what keepsakes she had of Rose. Accordingly, the miraculous statue of the Child Jesus, "The Little Doctor," was put on display, together with a rosary, some holy pictures, and other items. There was also a letter which Rose had written to Doña Maria some years before. The letter was signed "Rose of Saint Mary," the name so loved by Gaspar's daughter that she had taken it for her own the day she became a Dominican Tertiary.

Looking at the letter, Maria de Oliva recalled that far-off night when she had found her daughter fainting from hunger in her little garden cell. At the time she had wanted to send Marianna to a nearby store to buy chocolate and sugar with which to make a nourishing drink. But Rose had begged that Marianna should not be sent. In a few minutes, she insisted, a servant from the de Massa house would arrive with the hot chocolate already prepared, because she had asked her Guardian Angel to tell Doña Maria of the sudden attack of weakness.

"And so it happened," thought the mother. "In the middle of the night there was a great knocking at the garden gate. When I went to open it, there was the servant with a silver pitcher full of delicious chocolate. Rose drank it and felt so much better. The next day she wrote this letter to thank Doña Maria for her kindness."

Many other stories were told of Rose's gifts and virtues during the hours her body lay in state in Don Gonzalo's house. Several of these came from the Indian servant woman, Marianna. She, as well as Ferdinand (now a soldier in Chile), had shared many a secret with Rose. Faces paled as Marianna described Rose's heroic sacrifices, undertaken in the interests of sinners. For years she had worn a spiked metal crown under her white Tertiary veil; although, when the Jesuit priest, Father John de Villalobos, had heard of this unusual mortification, he had been so upset that he insisted on blunting most of the sharp points. Rose had also worn a chain about her waist, locking it in place, then throwing the key into the well near the back door.

"One night she couldn't stand this painful chain

any longer," said Marianna. "She sobbed and cried, and I knew I'd have to break the lock. But how, without waking the family?"

Her hearers were silent, absorbed in the picture of heroic generosity which her words painted so vividly.

"Go on, Marianna," said Father Alonso at last. "Explain what happened."

"The blessed child began to pray to the Mother of God, and the chain loosened of itself and fell at her feet!"

At the insistence of Father John de Lorenzana, a former Provincial of the Dominicans, Marianna continued to relate other stories about Rose's hero- ism. Finally Don Gonzalo requested permission to speak.

"I always knew Rose was a saint, Father John. Now, will you please look at this?"

The priest turned to take the paper Don Gonzalo handed him. It was a document, signed by Rose as she lay dying, requesting that the priests of Santo Domingo grant her an alms: she begged to be buried within the cloister of their convent.

"I felt every religious Order in Lima would want that holy body," Don Gonzalo hastened to explain. "In order to avoid trouble, I told Rose she would be practicing humility if she asked her Superiors in the Dominican Order to give her a burial place."

Father John de Lorenzana examined the paper carefully. There was no doubt that Rose's signature was authentic.

"It's nearly four o'clock," he said. "I wonder if

the body shouldn't be taken to Santo Domingo now. There are so many people crowding this house. At the church there would be much more room."

So presently Rose was being escorted through the streets of Lima for the last time. The crowds were so huge, so eager to obtain relics, that the soldiers of the Viceroy who had been guarding the de Massa house had to clear a way for the funeral procession. Everywhere—from balconies, from windows and doorways—men and women tried to get a last look at Gaspar's holy daughter. The air resounded with repeated cries as they begged Rose's blessing from her place in Paradise. Nor did anyone seemed surprised that the six pallbearers were members of the *Audiencia*, that very important group of men which assisted the Viceroy in matters of government. They knew that nothing was too good for *La Rosita*, their little Rose, who now was not only the pride of Lima but the pride of all Peru as well.

Slowly the immense procession made its way to the Dominican church. Gone were the usual distinctions between class and race. Spanish nobles walked side by side with Indian beggars. Negro slaves found themselves elbowing learned professors. Indeed, so dense was the crowd that Bartholomew Lobo Guerrero, successor to Turribius as Archbishop of Lima, had been unable to get to the de Massa house to head the procession. His carriage was forced to make a detour and await the body at Santo Domingo.

At the church, the holy remains were placed on

an elevated platform near the sanctuary. A small space was kept clear so that the sick might be able to approach and beg for cures. Rapidly the word spread that the body was warm and flexible, as though life still remained. And then there came a great cry of wonder as the Rosary Shrine, before which Rose had loved to pray, was seen to be bathed in a glorious unearthly light.

"Another miracle!" thought Father Luis de Bilbao, for fourteen years Rose's confessor. "The Mother of God herself pays honor to our little friend."

Because it was the Peruvian custom for burial to take place a few hours after death, preparations were soon being made to carry Rose's body into the convent cloister where a grave had been prepared. But such a cry arose from the people who had not yet secured a relic that the Archbishop consented to postpone the funeral. It would be held the next day, he said. In the meantime, the body would remain where it was, so that everyone might venerate it with due devotion. During the night it would lie in state in the novitiate chapel.

But the Archbishop's plan was to suffer a change. When dawn came, and the body was returned to the public church, the people of Lima refused to be parted from Rose. So loud was the chorus of tearful prayers that the celebrants of the funeral Mass could scarcely hear one another. The Bishop of Guatemala, Pedro de Valencia, could not believe his senses. How was he to conduct the ceremonies at the grave if such a hubbub continued?

LA ROSITA HAD BEEN PLEASED WITH HIS PRAYERS.

Finally another order was given: The funeral would be postponed for an additional twenty-four hours. At this good news a great wave of relief swept through the crowded church. People cried for joy. Now there was still a chance to claim a piece of the white woolen habit in which their dead friend was clothed, or one of the beautiful roses which encircled her head.

As the hours passed, excitement reached an even higher pitch. Everyone knew that several hopeless invalids had been cured after touching the holy body. One of these, a Negro lad of twelve years, was particularly in the limelight. He had been born with such badly crippled feet that he had never been able to walk. He could only drag himself along on his knees. Urged now by his great faith in the power of Rose's intercession with God, he had somehow managed to reach the elevated platform on which her body rested and had settled himself under it, behind the folds of the richly decorated black velvet pall. No threats could dislodge him from his refuge. In the end, *La Rosita* had been pleased with his prayers. She had granted him the normal use of his feet, so that he might walk, run and jump like other children his age.

"Look at the boy now!" said Don Gonzalo to his wife. "Did you ever see such joy in a child's face? Why, he's positively beaming! He's even helping other sick people to reach the body."

Doña Maria nodded. She had always believed that Rose Flores was a saint. Now she knew the whole world agreed with her, and her heart sang a *Te Deum* all its own.

But the Archbishop, Bartholomew Lobo Guerrero, was worried. As the hours passed, he sought
out the Prior of Santo Domingo.

"How many times has the body been clothed
with a fresh habit?" he asked. "Four or five?"

"Six times, Your Excellency. There's been an
enormous demand for bits of the habit as relics.
Many people have scissors hidden in their sleeves
and even the Viceroy's soldiers cannot keep all of
them from reaching the body."

The Archbishop nodded. "Then we'll have a
secret burial this afternoon, Father—during the
siesta. It's the only way."

The Prior realized the wisdom of the Archbishop's words. If the body of Rose Flores was not
buried soon, there was a chance it might suffer seri-
ous injury from the great crowds.

"A secret burial," he said slowly. "Yes, Your
Excellency. I'll see that everything is in readiness."

Promptly at noon the Dominican church began
to empty; soon each door could be locked and
bolted. No one showed surprise, for it was the
prevailing custom that everyone take a rest from
twelve o'clock until three. During these siesta hours
there was little activity anywhere. Churches and
shops were closed, and the shutters on each house
carefully drawn.

But this day there was no siesta at Santo
Domingo, nor did the Fathers of the community go
to dinner as usual. Instead, priests and lay Brothers
came in silent procession to the spot where Rose's

body was lying. Tall wax candles flickered as usual, and there was the same sweet fragrance of flowers. Once more the onlookers' hearts marveled at the beauty of this young sister in Saint Dominic who had been dead for thirty-six hours.

"Blessed be the day you came into the world," thought Father John de Lorenzana. "Pray for us, little Rose, now that you are in Heaven!"

The pallbearers stepped forward to take up their holy burden, and soon the procession had passed from the church into the cloistered garden of the convent. No sound was to be heard but the rustle of rosaries and the muted tread of the Fathers. This last farewell to Rose was of necessity a secret affair, lest the citizens of Lima learn what was happening and attempt to storm the church. But it was joyful nonetheless; there was happiness in every heart as Gaspar's daughter was finally laid to rest. A girl had died; a new saint now walked the courts of Heaven.

CHAPTER 13

HEROINES IN BLACK AND WHITE

IN THE months following her death, the fame of Rose Flores spread throughout South America. Each day hundreds of people came to Santo Domingo to ask her prayers. As the holy remains had been buried within the solemn cloister of the convent, however, no woman could enter to pray beside the grave. Finally, because of the increasing demand of Rose's friends, the Archbishop gave permission for the body to be moved into the public church. At this ceremony, which took place on March 19, 1619, some nineteen months after Rose's death, the remains were placed in a golden casket and set in a niche near the main altar.

The new site was not satisfactory, however. Crowds were continually coming and going through the sanctuary, even while the Holy Sacrifice was being offered. Finally the relics were moved again, this time to the shrine of Saint Catherine of Siena—a little chapel on the Epistle side of the main altar.

As the years passed, Maria de Oliva was amazed to find her position in society changing. No longer was she the simple wife of a man who made weapons for the Spanish armies in Lima. She had become an important person in her own right. Hardly a week passed that people did not come to pay her tribute, to congratulate her on being the mother of a saint. Many even left sizeable alms in gratitude for favors they had received after praying to Rose.

But the woman did not become proud. Her character had undergone a considerable change since Rose's death, and it was hard to believe she was the same person who had once ridiculed the Rule of the Dominican Tertiaries, and flown into a rage when told she would end her days wearing the habit of Saint Dominic's family.

"May God forgive me my many sins!" she often thought. "Dear Rose, pray for your poor mother!"

On February 10, 1624, the people of Lima flocked to the dedication of a new convent for women—the sixth to be built in the city. It was the Monastery of Santa Catalina, that had been foretold by Rose when she was living as a hermit in her father's garden. It was the first convent of Dominican nuns to be founded in Lima, and the tears flowed freely from Maria's eyes as she assisted at the Mass being offered in the new chapel. Her blessed child had been right. Father Luis de Bilbao was saying this first Mass. And in just a few minutes Doña Lucia de la Daga, whose husband and five children had died some years ago, and her young sister Clara, would kneel to receive the Dominican habit.

Within four years of its dedication, the Monastery of Santa Catalina sheltered one hundred and forty-five nuns. Soon this number increased to three hundred. Many priests, explaining the large number of vocations, stated that those already living behind the walls of Santa Catalina believed Rose Flores was in their midst. They felt she was helping them with her prayers, that she would make them saints. What wonder that Santa Catalina was flourishing? Not only was Saint Catherine of Siena its special friend and protector; Rose was watching over its welfare, too.

One afternoon, immediately after the nuns of Santa Catalina had finished chanting Vespers, a young lay Sister sought out the Prioress—once Doña Lucia de la Daga, now Mother Lucia of the Most Holy Trinity. The young religious wore a worried look.

"Sister Maria is worse, Mother. She's been calling for you all afternoon."

The Prioress looked up with surprise. "But she was so much better this morning, Sister! Doctor John de Tejada told me so himself."

The lay Sister sighed. "She's over seventy, Mother, and not too strong. I think you'd better come at once."

So Mother Lucia made her way to the tiny cell where the old Sister lay ill. Famous throughout Peru as the mother of Rose Flores, Sister Maria of Saint Mary had been a nun at Santa Catalina since 1629. But that was only four years—surely the good soul wasn't going to die yet!

Sister Maria thought otherwise, however. As the door opened and the Prioress hastened to her side, she raised herself on a feeble arm.

"Dear Mother Lucia, Rose said she would come to get me when I died. I think it will be tonight."

The Prioress fingered her rosary nervously. The lay Sister had been right: Sister Maria had suffered a change for the worse since morning. Her wrinkled face was now very pale and her breath came in labored gasps.

"But my dear, you mustn't say such things. Why not ask Rose for a cure? She's helped you before so many times."

"A cure? Why should I want that? I'm an old woman now, of little use to anyone. My husband is dead, my boy Ferdinand, my little Rose—ah, I just want to go to Heaven to be happy with these dear ones!"

There was silence in the little room as the sick woman fell back on her pillow. Mother Lucia looked down at the worn face, and a thousand memories rushed in upon her. The walls of Santa Catalina seemed to melt away and she was a young woman once again, a happy wife to Antonio Perez de Mondeja. Suddenly a girl's voice echoed in her ears:

"All this will pass away, Doña Lucia. Your husband and children will die. You will found the Monastery of Santa Catalina with your vast wealth. My own mother will seek the Dominican habit from your hands."

How impossible these words had seemed, back in 1614! Yet everything Rose had foretold was now a reality. Antonio was dead, their four sons and their daughter. Gaspar Flores had been called home, too. And the Monastery of Santa Catalina now gave praise to God by night and day.

Suddenly the sick woman opened her eyes. "Rose . . . Rose. . .where are you?"

Mother Lucia stretched out a soothing hand. "It's all right, my dear. Rose is in Heaven. Don't you remember? She's going to be canonized by the Holy Father."

Sister Maria shook her head. "I mean my granddaughter. Mother Lucia, could I see Mary Rose again? She. . .she reminds me so much of my own little Rose."

The Prioress nodded. "Of course you may see Mary Rose. And I'll call the others, too, if you wish."

"To say some prayers? Yes, I'd like that."

So presently the Sisters were assembled. The majority knelt in the corridor outside Sister Maria's room, but several gathered around the bed of the dying woman. All save one wore the habit of the Dominican Order. This was a girl of fifteen, in a simple black dress. She was Mary Rose Flores, whose father, Ferdinand, had died when she was very small. Upon her mother's death, the Governor of Chile, Don Francisco Lasso de la Vega, had sent her to Lima to be cared for by her grandmother. When the latter had entered Santa Catalina, Mary Rose had come along, too.

Affectionately the Prioress watched her make her

way into the room. She was a pretty child, the image of her holy aunt, but with one slight difference. She had a curious birthmark on one cheek—a tiny red rose. From the moment she had been born this birthmark had excited great curiosity. It was as though Rose Flores had set a sign upon her favorite brother's child, a sign which told that this little niece was already one of God's chosen souls.

"Come in, dear. Sister Maria wants to talk to you."

Mary Rose moved slowly toward the bed, her dark eyes wide with sudden fear. "You're not going to die, Grandmother? You're not going to leave me alone?"

Sister Maria smiled at the anxious young face. "I think so, my dear. But don't worry. These good religious will take care of you."

Mary Rose dropped to her knees. She mustn't cry. Her grandmother was going to Heaven. Didn't everyone in Lima know that Rose would lead her straight to the throne of God?

"You—you won't forget me?"

"Forget you? Of course not."

"But couldn't you live a little longer, Grandmother? Couldn't you wait to see me wear the Dominican habit?"

The dying woman smiled. "No, child. I'll watch that happy scene from Heaven. Ah, but you're lucky to have realized the worth of a religious vocation so young! Do you know what this foolish old woman said when Rose told her she would die a Dominican?"

The girl nodded. She had heard the story many times. Maria de Oliva had stated she would enter a convent only after she had seen an elephant fly.

"Yes, Grandmother. I remember. But you shouldn't tire yourself now. You should try to sleep."

The woman breathed a deep sigh. "You're right, child. I am tired. But don't go away. Stay here beside me."

Mary Rose put her hand in that of the dying woman, and for a moment there was a deep silence. Suddenly Sister Maria made an effort to speak.

"Mother Prioress. . ."

The latter stepped quickly forward. "Yes, my dear?"

"Ask the others to start praying, will you? I—I haven't much longer to live."

The foundress of the Monastery of Santa Catalina tiptoed to the open door and gave a signal. Immediately the nuns in the corridor and those inside the room began to sing the *Salve Regina,* that ancient chant sung by Dominicans whenever a fellow religious is dying. As the strains of the beautiful hymn filled the air, a bell tinkled in the distance. For the last time the chaplain was bringing the Blessed Sacrament to the mother of Rose Flores.

Sister Maria smiled. Her eyes, shining now with a new brightness, were fixed on some distant vision.

"Wait, Rose," she whispered, "not yet. . ."

Mother Lucia brushed back her tears. She was suddenly very happy. The air was full of a sweet fragrance now, that same fragrance which had filled the Church of Santo Domingo as the body of a saint had rested between tall funeral candles. And though she could not see the vision that rejoiced the heart of the dying woman, the Prioress knew the truth. A saint had come to keep a holy promise.

New York City
Feast of the Resurrection of Our Lord
April 25, 1943

By the same author...

6 GREAT CATHOLIC BOOKS FOR CHILDREN

...and for all young people ages 10 to 100!!

Also by the same author...

6 MORE GREAT CATHOLIC BOOKS FOR CHILDREN
...and for all young people ages 10 to 100!!

1200 SAINT THOMAS AQUINAS—The Story of "The Dumb Ox." 81 pp. PB. 16 Illus. Impr. The remarkable story of how St. Thomas, called in school "The Dumb Ox," became the greatest Catholic teacher ever.   4.50

1201 SAINT CATHERINE OF SIENA—The Story of the Girl Who Saw Saints in the Sky. 65 pp. PB. 13 Illus. The amazing life of the most famous Catherine in the history of the Church.   4.50

1202 SAINT HYACINTH OF POLAND—The Story of The Apostle of the North. 189 pp. PB. 16 Illus. Impr. Shows how the holy Catholic Faith came to Poland, Lithuania, Prussia, Scandinavia and Russia.   8.00

1203 SAINT MARTIN DE PORRES—The Story of The Little Doctor of Lima, Peru. 122 pp. PB. 16 Illus. Impr. The life and miracles of this Negro boy who became a great saint.   6.00

1204 SAINT ROSE OF LIMA—The Story of The First Canonized Saint of the Americas. 132 pp. PB. 13 Illus. Impr. The remarkable life of the little Rose of South America.   7.00

1205 PAULINE JARICOT—Foundress of the Living Rosary and The Society for the Propagation of the Faith. 244 pp. PB. 21 Illus. Impr. The story of a rich young girl and her many spiritual adventures.   10.00

1206 THE SET (Reg. 40.00)   30.00

U.S. & CANADIAN POST./HDLG.: $1-$5, add $1; $5.01-$10, add $2; $10.01-$30.00, add $3; $30.01-$50, add $4; $50.01-up, add $5.

Prices guaranteed through June 30, 1994.

CALL TOLL FREE: 1-800-437-5876

TAN BOOKS AND PUBLISHERS, INC.
P. O. Box 424
Rockford, Illinois 61105

MARY FABYAN WINDEATT

Mary Fabyan Windeatt could well be called the "storyteller of the saints," for such indeed she was. And she had a singular talent for bringing out doctrinal truths in her stories, so that without even realizing it, young readers would see the Catholic catechism come to life in the lives of the saints.

Mary Fabyan Windeatt wrote at least 21 books for children, plus the text of about 28 Catholic story coloring books. At one time there were over 175,000 copies of her books on the saints in circulation. She contributed a regular "Children's Page" to the monthly Dominican magazine, *The Torch*.

Miss Windeatt began her career of writing for the Catholic press around age 24. After graduating from San Diego State College in 1934, she had gone to New York looking for work in advertising. Not finding any, she sent a story to a Catholic magazine. It was accepted—and she continued to write. Eventually Miss Windeatt wrote for 33 magazines, contributing verse, articles, book reviews and short stories.

Having been born in 1910 in Regina, Saskatchewan, Canada, Mary Fabyan Windeatt received the Licentiate of Music degree from Mount Saint Vincent College in Halifax, Nova Scotia at age 17. With her family she moved to San Diego in that same year, 1927. In 1940 Miss Windeatt received an A.M. degree from Columbia University. Later, she lived with her mother near St. Meinrad's Abbey, St. Meinrad, Indiana. Mary Fabyan Windeatt died on November 20, 1979.

(Much of the above information is from Catholic Authors: Contemporary Biographical Sketches 1930-1947, *ed. by Matthew Hoehn, O.S.B., B.L.S., St. Mary's Abbey, Newark, N.J., 1957.)*